memory
training

memory training

Stop worrying about your memory
and start using it – to the full!

Jonathan Hancock

Prentice Hall
is an imprint of

Harlow, England • London • New York • Boston • San Francisco • Toronto • Sydney • Singapore • Hong Kong
Tokyo • Seoul • Taipei • New Delhi • Cape Town • Madrid • Mexico City • Amsterdam • Munich • Paris • Milan

PEARSON EDUCATION LIMITED

Edinburgh Gate
Harlow CM20 2JE
Tel: +44 (0)1279 623623
Fax: +44 (0)1279 431059
Website: www.pearsoned.co.uk

First published in Great Britain in 2011

© Pearson Education Limited 2011

The right of Jonathan Hancock to be identified as author of this work has been asserted by him in accordance with the Copyright, Designs and Patents Act 1988.

Pearson Education is not responsible for the content of third party internet sites.

ISBN: 978-0-273-74581-5

British Library Cataloguing-in-Publication Data
A catalogue record for this book is available from the British Library

Library of Congress Cataloging-in-Publication Data
Hancock, Jonathan, 1972-
    Brilliant memory training : stop worrying about your memory and start using it - to the full! / Jonathan Hancock.
        p. cm.
    Includes bibliographical references and index.
    ISBN 978-0-273-74581-5 (pbk. : alk. paper) 1. Memory. 2. Mnemonics. 3. Recollection (Psychology) I. Title.
    BF385.H2747 2011
    153.1'4--dc22   2011009435

10 9 8 7 6 5 4 3 2 1
15 14 13 12 11

Typeset in 10pt Plantin by 3
Printed and bound in Great Britain by Henry Ling

For Lucy, Noah, Evie and Nate

Contents

About the author

Jonathan Hancock taught himself to have a brilliant memory when he was still at school – to win a bet, and then to break two Guinness World Records. He was one of the first people to achieve the rank of Grandmaster of Memory and became World Memory Champion at the age of 22. He has since shown off his remarkable memory on TV and radio programmes around the world.

A graduate of Oxford University and former BBC radio presenter, Jonathan has published ten books on thinking and learning, acted as a memory consultant for broadcasting and telecoms companies and led training courses in business and education.

Alongside his job as a teacher in a busy city primary school, every year Jonathan works with The Learning Skills Foundation to run the national Junior Memory Championship.

A keen marathon-runner, he lives with his wife and three children in Brighton.

Author's acknowledgements

I'd like to thank Samantha Jackson, Rachel Hayter and the whole team at Pearson for their enthusiasm and support for this book from the start.

Thanks are also due to my agent, Caroline Shott, and to all the members of The Learning Skills Foundation.

And to my family: endless gratitude for the patience and consideration they've shown me during the writing of this book. They're a constant reminder of the fun, excitement and joy involved in laying down lasting memories, and my life with Lucy, Noah, Evie and Nate has given me so many rich experiences to remember and cherish.

Introduction

We used to believe that memories were made in our hearts. Then we discovered the brilliant brain, and the last few centuries have been spent trying to understand what's going on between our ears. But memory's on the move again. The more we try to pin it down, the more elusive it becomes. And I don't know about you but a great deal of my memory is now definitely in my back pocket.

Inside my mobile phone I have all the numbers I use regularly, plus access to online directories that let me track down anyone else I might need to call. The internet provides me with more information than I will ever have time to use, accessible wherever I am in the world. My phone itself holds lists of jobs to do, calendars full of important birthdays, daily schedules, email address lists, maps ... The alarm reminds me to wake up in the morning, the voice-recorder allows me to gather information on the move and retrieve it at my leisure, and the camera helps me to record and relive any moment I choose in phenomenal detail.

And yet ... I'm *so* glad I learnt to use my own memory power. It's changed my life, and I want this book to change yours.

There's never been a time when memory was more important. Thanks to the speed the world turns, the sheer amount of information hitting us from every angle, the increased demands on our time and energy, and the high standards we set ourselves for what we can do in a lifetime, memory is now a more valuable commodity than ever before. There may be more tools to support it, but there's so much more going on to challenge it, and there's no escaping the fact that your memory is still crucial to your success in everything you do. But it's not just about coping, forgetting less, stopping the rot. It's about making very conscious decisions to use memory to be brilliant. Your confidence with memory goes to the very heart of who you are and what you can achieve.

I've had some wonderful adventures with memory. I taught myself to memorise playing cards to break world records, then learnt how to remember *anything* to win memory awards and competitions ... and suddenly discovered a growing community of people fascinated by the latent power of the human brain. I found out about memory techniques that had been around since ancient times and which still worked today. In fact they were perfect for the modern world because they made it possible to remember at speed, under pressure, creatively, efficiently, enjoyably; and rather than simply remembering more, they revealed the importance of remembering *better*. Because these days it's not how much you can remember, but what you choose to do with your memory that really counts.

Anyone can have a better memory. It's an active skill that you learn and practise. Ancient civilisations were much more aware of the best systems and strategies, but there's no reason why you can't start using some powerful techniques immediately and get so much more out of your memory, however old you are and whatever your experiences of learning have been like so far.

You'll remember more – and do it faster, find it easier, be more accurate. You'll get more out of everything you learn, engaging with it on a whole new level. You'll see the advantages of putting your learning skills to work in areas you never thought of before, and enjoy benefits you didn't even connect with memory: better communication, improved relationships, stronger imagination, sharper decision making, more confidence all round. You'll feel good about the future, know how to make other people remember you, and redefine your own opinion about what you can achieve – when you put your mind to it.

My pocket memory's good, and I use it every day, but the memory I've built for myself is what makes the real difference to what I achieve and how I feel.

I've written this book to get you started on your own memory adventure. I want you to see just what a difference it makes when you know what memory is really about, and how to use yours, *brilliantly*.

PART 1

Foundations

CHAPTER 1

Switching on

The true art of memory is the art of attention.

Samuel Johnson

In this chapter you will learn:

- how this book works, and how to *make* it work for you
- why ancient systems are essential in a modern world
- techniques for assessing your current attitudes and abilities
- which aspects of memory will help you most, now and in the future
- the dos and don'ts of developing a brilliant memory

This book is a memory manual, and you need to know that from the start. You've got hold of it, opened it, started reading it … and now you need to make a conscious decision to *use* it – because brilliant memory is all about choice, action and practice. It's a different way of thinking and doing. There are old habits to break and new behaviours to develop, and you'll only get there if you pay attention and commit to the challenge from the start.

It's an ambitious training programme, but trust the process. You'll be amazed at how quickly you can change the way you use your brain, and how easy it is to start enjoying the benefits of a brilliant memory. Be confident. You've got everything it takes.

Did you know?

Neurons, the nerve cells in your brain, communicate their electrochemical signals through junctions called synapses, determining the way you think and remember. Patterns of connectivity form thoughts and handle memories, and the strongest memories seem to involve particularly rich connections. Your brain holds around a hundred billion neurons, each with an average of 7000 connections to other cells. Brains simplify some of their structures with age, but an adult still has up to 500 trillion synapses – plenty of scope for a lifetime of complex connecting and brilliant memory making.

Your unique brain

Your brain is utterly original, one of a kind. Even the visible folds on its surface are different from every other brain on the planet, and your individual experiences have built you a brain unlike any other. There will be aspects of your thinking that operate particularly well, and others that need some work; but *your* memory improvement is the complete focus of this book, so don't worry about comparing yourself with others. You can use their examples and insights, but this training manual will work only if you personalise it and make it about you.

⟋ brilliant exercise

Picture an elephant. That elephant is now unique. It will probably be similar to the one I'm imagining as I write this, and to the elephants that other readers create; but the exact size, shape, colour, sound, smell and everything else about that particular elephant are yours and yours alone. The way it moves, the look in its eyes and, crucially, the way it makes you *feel*: it's all personal to you and your imagination.

You'll be asked to use your imagination throughout this book, and when you do you need to relish the fact that the results will be different from everyone else's. In fact, the memory strategies will work only if you make them your own. Having a brilliant memory is all about creating powerful, personal connections; so, follow my suggestions to get you started, but build up your confidence in what your own powers of imagination can do.

Everything in this book is designed to offer direct help to *your* memory, *now*. Many of the examples and exercises are based on particular occasions, activities or professions, but they all have something to offer – because they all develop thinking tools that benefit everyone. You'll find out how to apply them to your own specific needs, but the most important thing is that you try them all out from the start, training your brain and developing the powerful mental habits that will revolutionise your memory.

Celebrate that your brain is different. Make the most of the way your particular model works. Tap into your strongest emotions, incorporate your interests and experiences and use all the objects, places and people around you as you set up systems for remembering everything. Remember: your imagination is as private as you want it to be. Nobody needs to know what goes on in your head as you switch on your creative brain and let it loose on your learning.

Learning with others

So this book is about you, but you're not in it alone. The training process is very much about all the other people you come into contact with along the way. Not only are you going to learn how to speak and write in ways that everyone else remembers, and to present yourself with a really positive impact, but you'll also be able to lead by example. The things you learn about memory can change the way all the other people in your life behave, think and remember.

And it's also about some important people from the past. This is a modern book that includes some very ancient wisdom: a unique combination of the old and the new. The memory strategies explored are relevant to all the real challenges you face, but they're all based on old-fashioned traditions. To build a brain capable of coping with today's demanding world you need to know how earlier civilisations mastered the art of memory.

Memory, then and now

These days, in techno-speak, SIM may stand for Subscriber Identity Module, that tiny card that stores key data on your phone. But Sim was also a very important man in the history of memory, and his story should help you to see why the ancient world has such a role to play in this modern memory manual.

 **example**

Sim's story

Like you, Sim was interested in memory and how it could benefit his life. He'd developed memory strategies to help him in his profession and was making quite a success of it, but it took a tragedy to bring about his breakthrough moment ...

Sim had been asked to give a presentation at a big social event, but he got into an argument when the host tried to get out of paying him the full fee. Just as things were getting heated, Sim was called outside: remarkable good fortune, really, because at that moment the roof of the building collapsed, crushing all those inside. The bodies were mangled beyond recognition. As the sole survivor, Sim was asked if he could help work out who was whom.

To everyone's amazement – not least his own – Sim found that he could remember every single person at the banquet simply by thinking about where they'd been sitting. The structure of the building provided the structure his memory needed, boosted by vivid images of the room mixed in with powerful emotions and a driving need to make his memory work.

Crucially, Sim used this experience to learn how to remember better. He recognised the things that activated his recall, and decided he was going to find ways to keep using his memory this brilliantly.

Sim is short for Simonides, the Ancient Greek poet in this seminal episode in the history of memory. The events described above took place at a feast organised by the rich businessman Scopas, who wanted Simonides to perform from memory but didn't want to pay him properly (although, in the end, he did pay the price …). Legend has it that Simonides' insights into the architecture of memory and the power of places and pictures set the ancient world alight, revealing how memory could be controlled and put to powerful use.

Throughout this book you'll be using lessons from the distant past to improve your success in the most modern scenarios. You'll need to know something of the history and a little of the science, but what you need most of all is 'guided practice': opportunities to feel what it's like to use your memory well *now*.

⟶ brilliant exercise

Have a go straight away. Experience how the ancients used to switch on their memories.

You're going to learn the following shopping list, in perfect order, forwards and backwards. Here's your first chance to learn how to remember by *doing* it.

rice   sausages   wine   peas   cheese   eggs   chicken   bin-bags
tinfoil   washing-powder

Look at the four corners of the room you're in now. In a moment they're going to be filled with shopping – thanks to the powers of your creative imagination.

Pick one of the corners and keep your eyes fixed on it as you imagine a large pile of rice there, with sausages sticking out. Superimpose this image on the real corner of the real room.

Then turn to the next corner, clockwise from the first, and this time picture a large glass of red wine there, with peas bobbing on the surface.

Turn again, and in corner number three imagine seeing a big piece of Swiss cheese, with a hard-boiled egg squeezed into each one of the holes.

In the last corner, imagine you can see some baby chickens jumping into the black bin-bag that's been taped to the wall. Really see this strange scene happening in front of your eyes.

Finally, in the very centre of the room, imagine that a large square of tinfoil has been laid down and covered in a thick layer of washing powder.

This is what Simonides did: he used the structure of a building to hold on to information for him. See if it's worked for you. Look back around the room and see if you can find the traces of imagery in each corner and in the middle. There should be two items of shopping in each of the five places, giving you the original list – in exactly the original order. And if you start with the product on top of the purchase in the centre, can you turn around the room anticlockwise and read out the ten items in reverse?

Opinions and beliefs

To start using the systems of the past you need to think about what your memory's like today, asking questions like:

- How good is it?
- What do you use it for?
- How do you feel about it?
- What are your current tactics for making it work?
- Which bits need the most support?

As you take your first steps along the path to a trained memory, it's important to spend some time thinking about where you are now and where you might go.

brilliant research

Several studies have estimated that around 80 per cent of our 'self-talk', about *everything*, is negative. There's probably a good evolutionary reason for this: our brains are designed for survival, and being cautious and sceptical is usually a safe bet. Learning new skills, thinking differently and stepping out of a tried-and-tested comfort zone will always ring alarm bells, activating safety messages framed as negative thoughts.

When you're switching on to memory training, it's vital that you challenge some of your instinctive reactions. The voice in your head may tell you not to push yourself, to keep doing what you've always done, to feel the fear ... but, *do it anyway*. Test yourself to see what you can really achieve.

brilliant question

... about your attitudes to memory

Respond to the following statements as honestly as you can. For each one, give yourself a rating somewhere between 0 (completely disagree) and 5 (totally agree). At the end of the book you'll be able to return to these responses and see if your attitudes have changed.

'I have a brilliant memory.' ☐

'Nobody really needs to have a good memory these days.' ☐

'My memory is getting worse.' ☐

'I'm happy to tell everyone I have a bad memory.' ☐

'I'm past the point in my life when I need to learn new things.' ☐
'I'll be embarrassed if I try to do things from memory – and fail.' ☐
'I have all the thinking skills I need to learn memory systems
and strategies.' ☐
'My memory annoys and frustrates me.' ☐
'I'm excited about taking risks and learning in new ways.' ☐
'I'd be happier sticking with the strategies I use now, even the
ones that don't work.' ☐

It's good for you to face up to these feelings and bear them in
mind as you work through the book. Keep challenging them, seizing
on to evidence that might change your opinion – and noticing
when your *feelings* about your memory skills do improve. The more
positive you feel, the more likely you'll be to push ahead, to take
risks and set new targets, and to find the strategies that work for
you.

? brilliant question

… about potential barriers to your success

Because of our negative instincts, memory training involves
breaking through some significant barriers. All the factors below
have an effect on everyone's mental performance, although the
story isn't always as straightforward as you might think. In fact,
some of these things could even improve aspects of your memory.
The important thing is how you feel about these issues, and how
you choose to tackle them. Too many people miss out on all the
benefits of a trained brain because they accept the negatives at
face value.

Spend the next few minutes thinking about the things that could
stop you building a brilliant memory. Remember, the important

thing to consider is what you *feel* might hold you back. Rank the ideas below, from 10 (the least problematic) to 1 (the biggest potential barrier for *you*).

Your age, and the effects ageing has on your memory. ☐
Previous habits: for good or bad, you're stuck with particular learning strategies. ☐
The limited time available to you to experiment and practise. ☐
Your education: either the ways in which it failed you or the hard-to-break habits you were taught. ☐
Your intelligence: surely you have to be very clever to develop a brilliant memory? ☐
A poor track record at learning new things. ☐
Health issues: specific physical or mental problems, or general tiredness, discomfort or infirmity. ☐
Low motivation, lack of inspiration, poor willpower. ☐
Weak imagination: I've heard the art of memory requires a very creative brain. ☐
Lack of bravery, fear of failure. ☐

As with the attitude statements earlier, you'll be challenging these ideas throughout the book. There's no escaping it, though: these factors do have power. Ageing alters your brain. The habits you've developed will affect your memory training. Time to put new techniques into practice is important ... and so on. But none of these issues has to be a dead-end, and many of them could actually become the secrets of your success.

Analysing your attitudes, fears and overall feelings about memory is a positive step in itself. You know where you're starting from and can begin to build your confidence – and to enjoy the very clear benefits that can have for your learning. Seize on anything that might shift the 'self-talk balance' in the positive direction.

The power of positive thinking

Deep down you know that you can do much more with your mind. You may not remember many of the billboards you passed in the street yesterday, because your memory isn't that good and you weren't paying attention and your mind isn't at its best right now and ... and ... and if you were offered a thousand pounds for every one you recalled, or if your life depended on remembering ten of them, how well do you think you might do then?

 research

When volunteers in a famous experiment were asked to learn a list of 100 foreign words, they did so with 92 per cent accuracy. But another group was given 200 words to study, and their success rate *increased*, to 97 per cent. And when the target number was upped to 1000 words, accuracy only dipped slightly, to 96 per cent – still clearly better than the original 100-word group. Expectation has great impact. Learn to expect more from your memory, set yourself higher targets and let your brain extend itself beyond the limits of old.

Did you know?

Your memory works best when you're happy. Research has shown that distractions of all kinds, including distracted thinking like fear and worry, significantly disrupt the learning process. Memory problems are key symptoms of depression, and children have been shown to learn much more in lessons which they enjoyed.

A day in the life of your memory

Mental imagery will become one of the most important tools in your memory kit – and here's another early chance to warm up your imagination. You're going to visualise a typical day in your life, focusing on the times when memory plays a part. Don't worry if this feels difficult. You'll be getting plenty of practice at exploring information in your mind's eye. Just start by picturing yourself going through an average day.

Start at the moment you wake up. *How* do you wake up? Does anything remind you it's time to get going? How soon do you normally start thinking about what the day might involve? Do you use any tactics or tools to help you remember what's in store?

brilliant tip

When you're imagining a scene like this, you might find it easiest to picture events unfolding from your own point of view, or to watch yourself from the outside, like a character in a movie. Get used to controlling the pictures that appear in your mind. Zoom in, pan round, find a wide shot or go for an extreme close-up. It's your imagination and you're in control.

As you follow the whole day through, stay alert for every time your memory is in use. When you've finished and your imaginary day has ended, spend a moment thinking about two questions: how did you use your memory, and how could you have used it better?

So, how many different acts of memory were involved?

It's likely that you had to remember what to do, bring, buy, finish ... how, when, why and where ... whom you were speaking to, what to say; and, afterwards, what you *said* and how you felt – because we all spend time reviewing experiences and reflecting on the past, not always very accurately. Too often memory is thought of in terms of details such as names, phone numbers and anniversaries, skills consciously learnt, or particular recall challenges like presentations, interviews and tests – and even your average day will have involved many of these demands. But there are also more subtle forms of remembering.

And what about the recall you take for granted, about family names, your own address, how to operate your car – plus that whole layer of memory that keeps your lungs going and your heart pumping ...? There are so many different memory systems in operation around the clock: some we stress about, others we rely upon, and many we have to think hard about even to spot.

You use your memory so much more than you realise. In your imagined day, when someone was speaking to you, did you consider the memory skills that let you hold their words in your head long enough to put them together into a sentence? Did you recognise how the smell of burning toast reminded you about the breakfast you'd started making? Did you think about the songs on the car radio that reminded you of the past?

Considering every single moment of memory is clearly a next-to-impossible task, but *trying* to should reveal how big a role memory plays in your life, and how well it works most of the time – another bit of positive thinking to bear in mind! But what about the things that could have gone better ...?

brilliant question

When could memory have helped you more?

Keeping aside those days when memory is in the spotlight (final exams, major presentations, wedding speeches …), you should have no problem spotting room for improvement even in a typical twenty-four hours.

Be honest: how often does your memory fail you for key details that could make all the difference? And even if you do remember most of them, how much more could you achieve if you knew how to manage everyday data faster and more reliably?

Would a better memory save you time and stress? What would it be like to have full control of all the information coming your way?

Would your targets be set higher if you were more confident about your memory? Might you do things differently, or take on completely new challenges?

How could memory skills improve your performance at work, in social situations, playing sports and games – even just around the house, sorting the DIY, shopping and finances, managing the family?

If you had a better memory, what might your life be like? Could it make you feel different about yourself?

Examining a typical day like this is a very useful activity, and it shouldn't stop here. Start noticing memory in your real life and deepening your answers to these two key questions. It's a vital early step in memory training because it helps you to learn about the memory techniques and habits you've developed, to reflect on what's working and what's not, and to highlight areas where memory could provide a big boost to your success. It's honest, realistic, practical and positive: everything that *Brilliant Memory Training* is about.

brilliant timesaver

It's important to make the most of every memory aid available, especially the modern ones that work so well. Don't even think about throwing out your address book, diary or personal digital assistant. It's how you use them that counts, and you'll see how they can work brilliantly alongside your trained brain. A key message throughout this book – to save time, to boost accuracy, to achieve more and just to make life easier – is to take all the help you can get.

Target setting

So with all those applications and potential benefits of memory fresh in your mind, it's time to decide just how good you want to be. Remember, you're challenging your natural negativity and setting ambitious goals because that's the way to make your brain raise its game. This is a memory users' manual, after all, designed to get you doing things differently and quickly enjoying the rewards.

Spend the next few minutes choosing your priority areas for improvement and imagining how things could change. The more detailed your targets, the more likely you'll be to hit them.

Target: *attitudes*

Which of your attitudes about memory do you most want to change? Look back at the list you considered earlier. Which three attitudes do you want to have shifted furthest by the end of the book?

Target: *barriers*

There are plenty of potential barriers to your memory training, some of which can be tackled practically and others that require a change in perception. Have another look at the list of potential barriers. Which three factors are your priorities to overcome?

Target: *applications*

Having thought carefully about the way you're using memory now, you should have some good ideas about where you could achieve more. Choose three specific uses of memory that you're going to focus on. You can still experiment with all the other areas covered in this book, but these will be your principal targets and key measures of progress.

Target: *benefits*

What about the more general benefits of memory training? Some important themes have already started to emerge, like organisation, confidence, creativity and ambition. Spend a moment looking back through this chapter and choose three areas to prioritise. Which benefits would most improve your life?

Target: *skills*

To train your memory you need to build 'foundation' skills like concentration, visualisation, even your sense of humour. So, which ones do you want to prioritise? Where do you think your brain is currently letting you down? Choose three skills to develop: either because they need the most work or because you think they might have the most to offer.

The new you

Many books would leave it there for now. But this one expects more, and you've already done enough careful thinking to go one step further. With all your targets in mind, spend a final moment building a 'memory' to live up to. Use every thinking skill you can muster to create a mental image of what your brilliant memory could do for you.

With your most influential attitudes corrected and the main barriers overcome, which memory activities will give you most practical help, satisfaction and pleasure? How will your wider mental abilities be improved? And what about the ripple effects on your core thinking skills?

↗ brilliant exercise

Choose one of your target applications. Whatever it is, picture yourself doing it brilliantly, using your memory quickly, easily, confidently. Before long you'll be combining your natural memory capacity with the *artificial* memory you're going to build – so imagine that happening now. You'll know how to get the most out of all the external memory aids at your disposal, combining them with your trained mental powers. In your imagination now, focus on how it would – how it *will* – feel to be that good: what it's going to do for your overall mental confidence. Make this picture detailed and clear. It's a great way to practise all the thinking skills that will underpin your brilliant memory, and to build a 'beacon' image to move towards that represents everything your brain can achieve.

✗ brilliant dos and don'ts

As you switch on your brain and click into the training, here are some important bits of advice that could make all the difference to your success. Like your memory itself, what you get out of this book depends largely on how you use it. So …

Do

✔ *Do ... give everything a go.* Try all the experiments, activities and exercises in this book. They're all designed to develop important skills. Even when a particular example doesn't seem to suit your needs, you might be surprised about what it has to offer you in similar situations – and the impact it can make on your general brain training.

✔ *Do ... try it out for real.* The challenges within this book are only the start. Take every opportunity to put memory strategies to work in your real life. Test them in the situations that are most important to you. Thinking habits are particularly ingrained, but they can be changed and you can set up much more effective ways of using your brain. The theories in this book will quickly make sense when you try them out for real.

✔ *Do ... be honest.* Reflect on which strategies are paying off, and which are not. Adapt and combine the different techniques, be clear about the things that need more work, but also celebrate the successes as your efforts start to bear fruit – possibly in some unexpected ways.

Don't

✘ *Don't ... be negative.* However you feel about your memory now, whatever your past experiences of learning and recall have been, wherever you feel you may have problems ... try to come to this book with an open mind. As Henry Ford said, 'Whether you think you can or whether you think you can't, you're right.' In memory training, a positive attitude and eagerness to experiment and improve are key ingredients of your success.

✘ *Don't ... focus on failure.* This book has been written to help you raise your game and to challenge you to achieve more. You wouldn't be here if you could do it all straight away. Some of the skills involved in memory development involve a major shift in your thinking, so prepare to feel your mental muscles being stretched – and to go easy on yourself if you can't do all the exercises immediately. Memory is a skill, and you'll *need* to make plenty of mistakes as you learn how to do it properly.

✗ *Don't ... look for excuses.* Age, health, experience, time, confidence: there are plenty of factors affecting your memory abilities, but they can all be managed to allow you to succeed. Turning them into excuses will stop you taking control of your memory and having the best brain possible. Set your targets high. You've seen the barriers to success: now you're going to train yourself to jump them.

 **brilliant** recap

- A brilliant memory isn't something you have, it's something you *do*.

- Take every opportunity to personalise the training, to make it work for you.

- Prepare to combine the latest technology with the oldest memory techniques.

- Challenge all your attitudes: to memory in general, and to yours in particular.

- Set ambitious targets for how you want memory skills to change your life.

CHAPTER 2

Memory building

Memory is the cabinet of imagination.

Edward M. Forster

In this chapter you will learn:

- what 'artificial' memory is all about
- the traditional tactics used to improve recall
- your place in the history of memory training
- how to assess your abilities in the core learning skills
- ways to start setting up your brain for memory brilliance

We've known how to build brilliant memories for thousands of years. Whenever memory has been valued and celebrated, memory *skills* have been developed to make the most of its power. The Ancient Greek dramatist Aeschylus called memory 'the mother of all wisdom'; in Rome, Cicero said that memory was 'the treasury and guardian of all things'; and both of these men lived at times when memory was worshipped like a god. Modern technology may accelerate and expand our mental powers, but previous generations knew the benefits of constructing *personal* memory capacity. They made sure that the art and artifice of memory were woven into the fabric of life.

Artificial intelligence

The distinction between 'natural' and 'artificial' memory is a really important one. It reveals how memory skills can revolutionise everything you do. It's tempting to assume that artificial means *technological*; but it's not as simple as the memory in your head versus the modern props and gadgets that support it.

brilliant definition

Artificial memory

This concept has actually been around for centuries. It doesn't refer to external aids, but to the things you can do *with* your brain: to the art of memory. Rather than just trusting your brain to keep hold of information, you make absolutely sure it does, by using strategies and systems. You consciously change the original material to *make* it memorable, then fix it inside the artificial mental structures you've built into your brain.

When the Roman orator Cicero walked around the rooms, hallways and courtyards of his imaginary memory buildings, he saw statues, vases and other delightful things, all carefully arranged and meticulously maintained. His mental journeys were relaxed and inspiring, each area light and airy, the places in his imagination rich but uncluttered, filled with just the right number of interesting objects. And each object was there for a reason: a carefully chosen symbolic clue to remind him of an important piece of real-life information. So, constructing arguments, teaching or speaking from memory – sometimes for hours on end – Cicero could walk around his imaginary architecture, find the items he'd put there, and trigger memories for every word, fact, name or idea he needed, all laid out in precise order.

Public-speaking was a big part of life in Rome and it became a very powerful advert for memory techniques. The Roman teacher and orator Quintilian said: '*We should never have realised how great is the power [of a trained memory] nor how divine it is, but for the fact that it is memory which has brought oratory to its present position of glory.*'

Before learning more about the glorious history of man-made memory, it's worth thinking about some of the artificial things you already do to help you remember. Here's a list of common techniques used today by people the world over, and they have a lot to say about the way memory works (or doesn't).

Typical tactics

Most of us collect a set of personal memory habits and strategies. Some we're shown, by teachers, friends or relatives; some we learn about in memory guides, from newspaper articles or television shows; others we just develop, by trial and error or through sheer chance. And when we find that something seems to boost our recall, we tend to stick with it.

See how many of the following habits you recognise. Give them all a rating: do you use them *very often, occasionally, rarely* or *never?*

Using the alphabet

To remember a name you run through the possible initials one by one. 'Did his secretary's name start with A, B, C ...? Yes, C: it was ... Carrie.'

brilliant exercise

How many random words can you name in 15 seconds? And then, how many random words beginning with P can you say in the same timeframe? Your score for these tests is likely to be very similar, and many people actually do better in the second test. Did you notice how much easier it felt when your memory had an initial letter to focus on? Language is such an important aspect of your mental filing-systems, and it makes sense to use the alphabet to help you retrieve stubborn memories.

Going back

It helps if you return to the last place you remembered something. You get to the top of the stairs, realise you've forgotten what you came up for, so go back to the kitchen where you probably had the idea – and, miraculously, you remember it again.

⌐ brilliant research

Physical spaces can act as strong anchors for memory. Research shows that recall can be boosted dramatically by re-creating the conditions in which something was learnt. It's why witnesses are often taken back to the scene of the crime or told to focus on memories of physical places and environmental conditions. Professor Alan Baddeley proved that divers were much better at remembering test information they'd learnt underwater when they were back underwater. Scientists also talk about 'state-dependent memory', referring to someone's state of mind at the time of forming a memory. Retrieving that memory tends to be much easier when they're back in the same state; and, since places can affect our mood, going back somewhere physically is often doubly significant as it helps to 'take you back' emotionally.

Following connections

Associations and mental links lead you to the answer. 'They've gone on holiday to somewhere hot, and it was in a TV show, and there were boats ... Aloha ... Hawaii!' Sometimes thinking backwards is the key, retracing your mental footsteps. 'We were talking about cakes because Lily had one specially made, and you'd asked why she was off work, because we were discussing ... that's it, your job hunting. So how's it going?'

Our memories are stored within an intricate web of connections. Neuroscience has demonstrated what we know from experience: that memories can be accessed from a number of

different 'directions', following connections from other memories and linking through imagery, language, senses, feelings …
Think of a moment in your life that you remember well and
think about often. What are the things that prompt you to go
back there in your memory? How many different thoughts
might remind you of it? Could you get to wherever it is in your
brain through a smell, a colour, a particular word, a feeling,
another memory?

brilliant tip

It's great exercise for your memory to follow these associations and
connections whenever they crop up. The next time a seemingly
random memory pops up, do some detective work. What made you
think of that moment at *this* moment?

Leaving reminders

*You leave your bag by the front door, move a chair to stop you
touching the broken desk or tie a knot in your handkerchief to remind
you that you have something to remember.*

Our brains are very good at spotting things that are out of the
ordinary: in particular, items that don't fit the rest of a pattern.
It's known as the *Von Restorff effect* – named after scientist
Hedwig von Restorff, who showed that it's much easier to
remember a bit of information that's different from the rest. So
making one corner of your handkerchief look different, placing a
bag across the doorway to disrupt your normal movements and
writing out key information in different colours are all likely to
help you remember.

Striking a pose

Somehow scratching your head, rubbing your chin or looking up at the sky helps you remember.

It's fascinating to look at people's eye movements when they're trying to remember something. The eyes tend to follow particular patterns depending on the type of memory being accessed – a phenomenon studied by enthusiasts of NLP, neuro-linguistic programming, who analyse it to explore how we form mental models of our experiences. Try it yourself …

brilliant exercise

Remember something visually (what did your first house look like?) and your eyes (at least most people's) will go up to the left. In fact it can feel really hard to visualise a memory if you look anywhere else. *Invent* an image, on the other hand, and your eyes will go up to the right – so watch someone's eyes the next time you want to know if they're describing a real visual memory or one they've made up!

● Remember a sound (what does your ring-tone sound like?) and you look sideways to the left.

● Remember a sense or feeling (what was it like when you injured yourself?) and your eyes go down to the right.

The next time you find yourself adopting a particular pose when you're struggling to remember, ask yourself why. Does it help you mentally, letting your brain work in a particular way? Does it make you more comfortable physically, helping you to relax or be more alert or breathe more easily? Does it comfort you emotionally, perhaps reminding you of a particular pose or physical habit from childhood? Maybe it distracts you, gives you something else to think about – and makes space for the memory to pop back into your head? Or perhaps it signals to other people that you're thinking and buys you a bit of extra time!

Using pictures

You close your eyes and imagine a place, person or scenario as clearly as possible. You might even be able to picture your lesson notes or important pages from the textbooks you've used.

You'll find that the power of pictures is a central theme throughout this book. Many of our memories come with clear images attached, so it makes sense to explore them that way. Visualising information helps you to focus on it and carry out some of the other tactics in this list. And you quickly start up a kind of mental dialogue, because visualising seems to be strengthened by *verbalising*. It's like you're discussing an image with yourself as you see it in your mind's eye, enriching the visualised version as you explore the details, facts and ideas about it that you consciously remember.

🡵 brilliant exercise

Picture your first school, for example (did your eyes go up to the left?), and you'll probably find yourself reconstructing the images by talking things through in your head. 'We always came in through the main doors. The cloakroom was tidy because we didn't have big bags back then. The classroom belonged to … Mrs Brown, and her coat always hung on a hook by the door …' They say that a picture paints a thousand words, but maybe it's really the other way round!

Telling stories

You remember how to tie knots thanks to stories of pirates criss-crossing islands and rabbits going down holes. You turn initial letters into funny scenes and stories. You know how to spell 'because'... because Big Elephants Can't Always Use Small Exits.

Information becomes easier to remember when it has meaning, when it's patterned and connected and gives you some kind of story to follow – especially when that story is exciting, unusual, funny, rude … You'll be making use of these creative principles throughout your memory training, continuing a tactic that seems to come naturally. Long before written language, we used stories to retain information, and even now we rely on them to structure our thinking and strengthen our memories. We often add stories to what we're saying to make sure other people remember it. You'll see later that there's a right way and a wrong way of telling memory stories, especially when you're inventing one of those memory sentences for spellings or lists; but story-telling in general is a very effective strategy for almost every kind of memory challenge.

---

brilliant exercise

You can use the stories you know to store new information that you want to learn. For example, have a go at learning seven items to pack for a holiday by thinking of a day in the life of a girl called Goldilocks …

You *must* remember to bring:

camera   sunglasses   passport   sun-cream   books   hiking-boots
insect-repellent

So, you tell yourself a familiar story with some new details added.

> Goldilocks was wandering through the woods with her brand new camera, taking pictures of flowers, trees, animals – and the little cottage

she found. The cottage was painted bright white: so dazzlingly white, in fact, that she had to wear sunglasses as she approached the door. She took out her passport (what a terrible picture of her!) in case the owners of the house wanted some ID, but there didn't seem to be anyone in. So, she left her passport on the step and walked inside – only to find that the front room of the cottage was swimming in sun-cream, floods of it, sloshing around the floor and up the walls. To her relief she saw three books floating on the surface – one big, one medium and one tiny – and she managed to pull them together and use them like a raft, until the sea of sun-cream started to drain away, leaving her sitting on the floor next to three pairs of hiking-boots. Whose were they? She had a look and a prod and a sniff – and the smell told her immediately that the boots belonged to bears. She pulled out her insect-repellent and squirted the boots, herself, and the whole room around her, hoping it would also work to repel any large hairy animals who might be about to return home …

Now tell yourself the same story from memory and see how many of the holiday items you can find. Your brain should respond very well to this style of learning. Each bit of the story connects you to the next, and there's no reason why you couldn't have included many more images to trigger many more memories as the story went on, and on, and on …

Hearing rhythms

Do you find it easier to remember phone numbers if you say them in a particular way? Did you learn the alphabet, history dates or science facts using rhythms and rhymes?

Rhythms and rhymes are effective ways of giving information the pattern and structure it needs to stick in your mind. They also get you *doing* something to remember: tapping, clapping, singing, pronouncing words loudly and clearly – all of which helps you to hold on to your material in the short term, and to embed it for longer-term storage.

🔎 **brilliant** exercise

Read through this excerpt from a famous poem about the kings and queens of England. Learning it would help you to retain a great deal of historical information, but the key thing to notice at this stage is how naturally you emphasise the *rhythm* of each line. The fact that it's such a rhythmical poem is fundamental to its power.

Willie, Willie, Harry, Stee,
Harry, Dick, John, Harry Three,
One Two Three Neds, Richard Two,
Harrys Four Five Six … then who?
Edwards Four Five, Dick the Bad,
Harrys twain, Ned six the lad,
Mary, Bessie, James you ken,
Then Charlie, Charlie, James again …

Feeling your way through

You can type your PIN into the machine, or remember which buttons open the security door at work – but only by actually doing it. You use the pattern of physical movement: the way a particular memory feels.

Look out for these examples of 'muscle memory' in your life. They can be very positive habits, allowing you to slip into particular patterns of movement that produce good results – like the right door code or a powerful golf-swing. But be careful …

☀ **brilliant** tip

Always have another way of remembering something, so that you're not completely reliant on how it feels. If muscle memory is all you've got to go on, when it doesn't quite click you can suddenly be lost – and then, as too many golfers know, conscious thought only makes things worse. But you can disrupt these memories on purpose. Put your kettle in a different place tonight and, in the morning, when you reach for it automatically and find it's moved, you'll remember this bit of the book!

Making it personal

You're always on the look-out for connections with you: your age on a car number-plate, your first name in a newspaper article, your house number on someone's customer reference.

These things stand out as meaningful, important, unusual, interesting, fun – all important factors in making your memory work brilliantly.

brilliant exercise

Imagine you wanted to learn the following ten numbers: perhaps houses to deliver to on the High Street, catalogue order codes or important pages in a revision textbook.

2   37   14   29   25   54   37   16   61   88

One idea would be to link them all to you, to make the most of the power of personalising – and there are several ways you could do it.

First, take each number in turn and ask yourself the following question: *why is this the perfect number to describe me at this moment?* Some numbers really might be appropriate (it's my age, the temperature right now, the number of kids in the car), but for most of them you'll have to use your imagination and invent some personal significance.

37: because it's precisely the number of times I'm going to think about my boyfriend today.

25: because that's the number of people who could squeeze into that cupboard: five along, five across.

16: because it's half my house number: maybe just the bottom floor.

88: because last night I 'ate' and 'ate'…

Every good learning strategy and system relies on personal connections – using them if they're there, inventing them if they're not – and remember: this book began with a message about personalising every activity to make the training work for you, so it's a good idea to latch on to any available connections to you and your real life.

Another simple technique would be to imagine that these numbers represented *you*, at different ages. Flash a picture into your head of you as a two-year-old. What did you look like? How did you speak, eat, move? Now see yourself aged 37. What's your appearance like in this picture?

When you've gone through the whole list, cover up the numbers and see how many of them come to mind now. What sort of personal connections work best for you?

These are just ten of the many tactics we use. They're all effective techniques at times, although some are often used badly, and a few can occasionally hinder more than they help. Considering your own typical tactics gives you a glimpse of the way your unique brain works, highlighting the habits to keep as well as the skills that need attention; but there's also important evidence here about how memory works in general. Many of these typical tactics will return as you learn how to get the very best out of your brain.

 brilliant timesaver

Sometimes the best tactic of all is simply stopping, taking a break. You make a conscious decision to leave the remembering until later – and then the memory pops back when you're busy doing something else. Try it now. How many *Simpsons* characters can you name? (Or football teams, *Bond* movies or states of America?) Run through all the ones you remember straight away, but as soon as you come to a gap, stop. It's particularly good if you can stop while there's a memory 'on the tip of your tongue'. Tell yourself you're going to keep working on it in the back of your mind, but don't think about it consciously. See if the missing information comes back of its own accord, while you're reading about the history of artificial memory …

To make the most out of your memory now, you need to see how it *used* to be done.

Ancient masters of memory

The Greek poet Simonides is credited with inspiring great thought-leaders like Aristotle to explore and extend memory techniques. He'd spotted that places helped him to remember, which opened up an interesting new avenue in brain training; but he was already part of a poetic tradition of using memorable imagery, and Aristotle just continued investigating the ways in which artificial thinking could boost memory.

Memory skills through the ages

In the Middle Ages, memory systems were focused firmly on moral and religious activity. It was useful to have ways to remember the rules of behaviour and core aspects of belief. The groundwork of the Greeks and Romans now proved very helpful for honing meditation skills and developing powerful ways of reading and remembering religious texts. 'Illuminated' manuscripts contained a vivid mix of words and pictures, and even the non-religious poets and writers were eager to use memory techniques to make their offerings as memorable as possible.

The art of memory was developed throughout the Middle Ages. By the Renaissance, it was a key feature of visual art and public drama, and it even had a theatre of its own, invented by the sixteenth-century Italian Giulio Camillo. When you went inside his 'Theatre of Memory' you stood on the stage and looked out at objects and images arranged amongst the tiered levels before you, carefully organised and displayed to be memorable. Visitors were expected to use memory alone to get this visual 'download' of valued knowledge – just as audiences for Simonides' poems, listeners to Cicero's speeches, meditating medieval monks, Chaucer fans and Renaissance consumers of the arts could all be expected to use their 'artificial' memory skills.

So … what's happened to the art of memory since? Artificial memory mechanisms are still present in many of our festivals, with plenty of images, objects, rituals, songs and dances used to help us remember and repeat. Our writers, poets, artists, advertisers, politicians and propagandists all know the buttons to press to switch on our memories and make their material stick.

But somewhere along the line the active art of remembering seems to have been … well, *forgotten*. We have no shortage of modern memory aids, but the artificial memory *skills* cherished in ancient times and developed through the ages have fallen into a pretty bad state of repair.

Thinking skills

To take control of your memory, you need to train some key aspects of your thinking. So, how confident do you feel now about your concentration, organisation, visualisation, imagination, creativity and sense of humour? These are all vital components of a brilliant memory, essential skills for all the memory strategies and systems you're going to try, so spend a few moments reflecting on each of them in turn. Answer the questions honestly and have a go at a few quick experiments to help you judge your abilities right now.

Concentration

How well can you focus on a learning task? Do you concentrate well when memorising foreign words, learning lines for a play or watching a cookery demonstration – or do you get distracted and let your mind wander? How many of your learning projects do you actually finish?

↗ brilliant exercise

You'll need a watch, clock or mobile phone timer for this test. See how well you can estimate particular amounts of time. Start with thirty seconds. Set the timer going, then close your eyes and focus on the passing seconds. Count in Mississippis or elephants or whatever if you want, and see if you can say when thirty seconds have passed. Gradually extend your time targets, estimating one minute, ninety seconds, two minutes or even more. See if you can do it without saying a word. What difference does it make if you keep your eyes open? How about trying this test in a busy room? Can you imagine a clock with the second hand turning or the digits changing, to help you keep track of the count and improve your accuracy, however distracting the conditions?

Organisation

Is your approach to learning ordered? Do you make use of lists and clear plans of action? When you're studying for a test or preparing to give a presentation, do you spend time arranging your notes, resources and ideas? How organised is your mind?

⬈ brilliant exercise

Have a go at organising some familiar information. Can you list the seven days of the week in alphabetical order? It might help to imagine them written down, or to visualise a diary or calendar and see the days swap places as they slot into their new order. Can you sort them out logically, check you've considered them all, and read out the new order of days from the list in your mind?

Visualisation

How strong are your powers of visualisation? Can you view clear images in your 'mind's eye' to help you remember? When you try to put faces to names or explore memories of the past, do mental pictures figure in your thinking?

⬈ brilliant exercise

Here's a surprisingly tricky test of your visualisation skills. It involves bringing to mind something you've seen many times: an ice-cube. Imagine you've attached a thread to one corner of the cube and you're dangling it in your drink, keeping half above the surface. The question's this: as you look from above, what shape does the cube make in the liquid? Give yourself a moment to form the picture in your mind and examine it from different angles. Would it be easier if the cube was a die or a foldable frame? And once you've got an answer, what would you do with your mental image to check you're right? Could you expand it, unfold it, slice it ...?

Imagination

Can you go one step further and produce images of your own: new versions of realistic ideas, or completely off-the-wall concepts that could exist only in your mind? Do you use imagination to explore problems, visualise solutions and create helpful memory triggers? Could you transform programming instructions, complex formulae or dull lecture notes into something much more appealing, much more memorable?

brilliant exercise

Start with a mental picture of your home, and see what you can do with it in your imagination. First, think how you could transform it, if money was no object. See the place changing, developing into somewhere bigger, more luxurious, more exciting, more fun ... And then, to test out your imagination, what if the laws of science themselves no longer applied? Now anything's possible – so what images can your imagination offer?

Creativity

As well as visualising familiar pictures, can you create new ones? Can you add memorable images to help you learn directions, essays, sports skills? When you've got a problem to solve, how creatively can you manipulate memories, combine and extend them, and view the possibilities from different angles?

brilliant exercise

Try this challenge to your creative thinking. There aren't really any right or wrong answers, just as many interesting ideas as your mind can conjure up. How many ways could you use chocolate to improve the working life of your employees? You could give them all free chocolate ... but what else could you do with it? Can you think of ten original ideas? Twenty? More?

Humour

How often do you use your sense of humour and understanding of comedy to activate your learning? You know you remember funny moments, but do you *use* humour to learn recipes, to-do lists, foreign languages? Does it influence the way you communicate, teach, or make others remember you?

↗ brilliant exercise

Here are three quick exercises to test your sense of humour and comedic skill.

Number one: list five comedians that make you laugh. Picture them, recall their jokes, remember the way they make you feel.

Number two: think about five moments in real life that still make you smile. Were they surreal, embarrassing, surprising? How powerfully can you re-create them in your memory?

Number three: can you write funny answers to the following jokey questions: What did the foot say to the sock? Why is a teacher like a pot plant? What do you get if you cross a computer with a chocolate cake?

As well as helping you to analyse your current abilities, all these questions and examples are designed to switch on the key memory-building bits of your brain, and to deepen your understanding of what brilliant memory involves. You'll be getting more powerful training tips in the next chapter; and, by using these thinking skills to strengthen your memory, you'll find that you stretch and sharpen them all in return. You set yourself up to improve at all the memory challenges you've tried before, but you should already be spotting some new ways in which memory could make a big difference in your life.

brilliant recap

- Artificial memory techniques boost what the brain can do naturally.

- Think about the things you already do to improve your recall.

- Start extending your 'typical tactics' and make more of them in your learning.

- The training you've begun is part of a long and noble tradition.

- To have a brilliant memory, you need to strengthen all your core thinking skills.

CHAPTER 3

Memory boosting

The difference between false
memories and true ones is the
same as for jewels: it is always the
false ones that look the most real,
the most brilliant.

Salvador Dali

In this chapter you will learn:

- how to train the thinking skills that will maximise your memory
- what we know, and what we don't, about the human brain
- the life-spans of different types of memory
- why you remember and why you forget
- new ways to start forgetting less and remembering *everything*

It's time to start using your brain better, to create artificially brilliant memories of everything. As you discovered in the last chapter, some of your current memory methods are paying off, so keep doing anything that helps. But you also need to try out new ideas – and you're about to take a very different approach to a whole range of learning challenges, examining what your brain does when it works best and starting to change your approach to match. Give everything a go, develop strategies and systems that suit your brain and your life, and prepare to feel your memory doing some new and exciting things.

Change your mind

There's a famous saying that goes like this: *if you always do what you've always done, you'll always get what you always got*. Albert Einstein once said that the best definition of insanity is doing the same thing over and over again, but expecting the results to be different …

Chapter 2 identified the six key areas of thinking that contribute to having a brilliant memory. You're about to start using them all as you change the way you learn for ever; and so, to give you the very best chance of success, here's a mini training session for each one.

Concentration

To start training your concentration, why not try counting backwards at the same time as counting forwards? Out loud, count 'one, two, three …' up to ten, and at the same time *visualise* the numbers from ten down to one. So as you say 'one' you picture ten, on 'two' you see nine, and so on. Can you do it up to and down from 20, 50, 100? What happens when you carry out the two counts at different speeds?

You can also train your brain to concentrate with words. See if you can make up some meaningful sentences in which every word starts with the last letter of the previous one.

'I'm making good decisions.'

'After reading, get testing – go on, now!'

'How will Lisa and Diane enjoy your recollections?

It's a brilliant boost for your concentration, especially as you have to think of several things at the same time: the sentence so far, the last word, the last letter, the next word … And how easy do you find it to concentrate on something logical while you're also trying to be creative? To have a brilliant memory you'll need to be able to operate many different bits of your brain at once.

Organisation

You can easily start to train your 'organised thinking' skills. When you create memory sentences, for example, using the initial letters of words in a list, get into the habit of reorganising them to make remembering easier.

Here's a list of different types of energy:

gravitational   electrical   heat   light   chemical   kinetic

For once the order of the items isn't important, so why not organise them in a way that helps your memory? My wife's called Lucy, so I might decide it's useful to have her at the start of the sentence: *light* (L for Lucy). I could put *electrical* and *kinetic* next, to give me 'electric kettle'; and then what about reordering the last three words as *heat, chemical* and *gravitational*: '... heats cold gravy'.

Lucy's electric kettle heats cold gravy. It's a very memorable image. I can see it, touch it, hear it, smell it, taste it ... and now I have a much better chance of remembering those six ideas, thanks to some careful organisation at the start.

Often, the act of organising information (focusing on it, exploring it, doing something with it) is enough to make it memorable. That's particularly true when you *categorise* rather than just rearrange, and it doesn't seem to matter what categories you use – even ones you invent.

Try it yourself. Read this list of Christmas presents and group the items into categories of your choice, real or imaginary. For example, there's a group of foods in this list and a set of round things; but maybe there are also 'the three things that Neil Armstrong tried to smuggle to the moon', or 'items in the President's pocket' ...

ham   robot   watch   vase   torch   perfume   remote-
controlled car   aftershave   wine   tie   bowl   camera   mug
necklace   cheese

Now cover up the list and see how much of it stuck in your memory. If your organising and categorising has worked, one word should quickly trigger several more, and the categories themselves should be easy to remember because each one has several words to act as triggers. Which categories worked particularly well? If anything slipped your mind, how might you have connected it more memorably to the other items in the set?

Visualisation

As well as strengthening your visualisation skills, this exercise will provide you with a useful piece of memory 'equipment'. You're going to build yourself an item of mental furniture to hold your memories.

Visualise … a beautiful oak cabinet. It has two doors at the front which open to reveal three drawers on the left, three on the right, and two open shelves in between. See this piece of furniture as clearly as you can in your mind's eye. Walk around it, look at it from close up and from far away and build a very clear picture of it in your mind. Imagine opening the doors and checking that each drawer on the left is empty, then the top and bottom shelf, and finally the three drawers on the right.

Now you can put in some memories. Here's a list of eight countries that you want to talk about at a meeting, in this precise order:

France   China   Australia   India   USA   Italy   England Egypt

For each country, imagine you've been given an intricate little model of one of its famous buildings or landmarks. Then, gently and carefully, put the models into your cabinet: one in each of the three drawers on the left, one on each shelf, and then the remaining three models in the drawers on the right.

You might see yourself putting a model of the Eiffel Tower in the first drawer; then part of the Great Wall of China in the drawer below, followed by Sydney Opera House in the one beneath.

Carry on until you've visualised a model for each of the countries, and all eight models are safely inside. Practise seeing them in their individual spaces and as part of a whole collection of information.

And when you cover the printed list and open the doors of the cabinet in your mind, what can you see …?

Imagination

More than just seeing images vividly, you need to be able to transform them memorably in your mind. Imagination is at the heart of artificial memory; and the good news is that you can train it to be brilliant.

You can practise by changing dull, lifeless, forgettable information into something so rich and real that it already has a good chance of being remembered. You use your imaginative skills consciously and strategically to manipulate information, bringing it to life in your mind in unusual and ambitious ways.

Your next challenge is to change each of the following words into something that will excite your interest and activate your memory.

book   coat   tree   car   plate   apple

As words on a page they're pretty flat and uninteresting – but your imagination will soon see to that.

First, play around with the size and shape of each object. The book could be the biggest in the world. The coat might be only just big enough for an ant to wear. Perhaps the car is the longest stretch limo in history; the plate octagonal; the apple flat enough to post under a door. Picture all the images in your mind's eye and get used to using imagination to make them special.

Next, add one unusual detail to each picture. Use all the five senses imaginatively. What's odd about the way the book looks?

What strange noise does the coat make? Does the tree feel funny, or smell of something, or even have a memorable taste if you imagine biting into its bark …?

Now use your imagination to make each item *do* something memorable. You could pick a theme: for example, how would they all fly, or dance, or talk? If you focused on flying, the car might use its doors as wings, the plate could be fitted with helicopter blades, and perhaps the apple would burst high into the sky like a rocket? Or, forget about a theme and make all the actions different, creating five very memorable items with their own individual skills.

After all of that, it shouldn't be hard to remember the five items – and not just the original words, but all the rich, imaginative layers of detail you added. Holding them in your mind in this heightened form boosts your memory, but it also gets you engaging more closely with the information, so that *remembering* it is just the beginning of what you can do.

Creativity

Brilliant memory involves creativity on a number of different levels. You pick and choose from a range of strategies. You find creative ways to organise, visualise and re-imagine information. You invent clever images to remind you of complex or abstract ideas. And, as a result, you start using your memory to *boost* your creativity. You're motivated and alert, thinking in pictures and patterns, and able to bring together knowledge, experience and a wealth of new observations and ideas to produce some truly creative results.

---

brilliant exercise

Practise your creative thinking skills by finding images to represent the following bits of information: random words picked from a dictionary. Use the way the words look, how they sound, any associations that come to mind, and every other possibility that opens up when you inject creativity into your learning.

velocity   total   happy   eighteen   torque   permission

What image 'says' *velocity* to you? A cheetah, a jet plane, Usain Bolt? And what about this particular word, which could be easily confused with 'speed' or 'fast'? Maybe the plane is jetting over *Velo City*, home to the fastest animals and humans on earth?

Total is another abstract idea, so perhaps you make it as bright and exciting as a telethon 'totaliser', getting huge cheers at it's used to announce the latest total; or just break it down into a cute little boy: 'tot Al'.

You might picture a happy hippie … 'a teen' becoming eighteen … whatever combination of real meanings, creative associations and clever word-play produces the image clues that your memory loves.

And what about some names? Here are five Roman goddesses. If you wanted to learn them, for a talk, a test, or just to strengthen your historical knowledge, you'd need to turn them into images – and you'd have to think very creatively to come up with the pictures to use.

Vesta   Terra   Ceres   Minerva   Venus

Is Vesta only wearing a *vest*? Is Terra acting like a *terror*? Maybe Ceres *cares*, Minerva works down a *mine*, Venus loves exotic *venues* …?

This creative interpretation of the material gets you well on the way to remembering it brilliantly. And when you've got your five images, why not spend a moment trying to organise them creatively, connecting them together somehow to keep them in your mind. Is there a clever way you could order them, categorise them, combine them into a single scene or link them into a story?

Humour

It's probably not possible to train your sense of humour (although you could explore some different types of comedy, mix with funnier people and find more opportunities to relax and laugh), but you can definitely practise *using* comedy to activate your memory.

↗ brilliant exercise

Here are two ideas to try. First, take the following famous names and put them into a funny story involving every kind of visual comedy you can imagine. Steal ideas from all the comedy films you've seen. Use slapstick, surprise, practical jokes, farce, coincidence, misunderstanding … anything you can think of to raise a smile.

Mickey Mouse   Elvis   Napoleon   Madonna   Harry Potter   Dumbo Arnold Schwarzenegger   Oprah Winfrey   Dracula   Pelé

Maybe Mickey Mouse slips on a banana skin and lands on top of Elvis in the middle of a song – and he jumps into a cupboard where Napoleon has accidentally covered Madonna and Harry Potter in custard …

Visualise the events being played out in front of a packed audience, and exaggerate the sound of their laughter at each moment of madness.

And as a second exercise, what would happen if your favourite comedian became your teacher? Choose a famous comedy star, past or present, and then imagine them giving you the following information (the directions your friend's just given you to the party tomorrow night). How would Bill Cosby, Charlie Chaplin, Joan Rivers or Laurel and Hardy tell you to go …

… up the hill as far as the church, then right on to the main road for 12 miles. When you get to the garage, take the next left, go past the factory, under the railway bridge and then right at the school. The house you want is number 88, with a blue door.

A key component of comedy is exaggeration, so make sure your chosen comedian supplies you with extreme examples of their distinctive style. Imagine them pulling out all the stops to find humour even in some dull driving instructions. How would they make them funny – and make you remember them?

brilliant impact

British comedy star Al Murray says he finds it hard to remember new people he meets at parties. But when he's on stage, even working at speed and under great pressure to perform, he's able to interact with the audience and remember many of their names. He turns them into new characters for his act, finds comedy in their names, jobs, hobbies, opinions … and he can remember them all with ease. Making things funny simply makes them more memorable.

Your brilliant brain

You'll be getting many more opportunities to stretch these skills as your memory training continues. Your new approach to remembering relies on them. You'll be constantly exercising the core aspects of your thinking – and you'll need to, because memory is a complex process. We've been struggling to understand it for millennia, and exploring a little of the history now will tell you a lot about what you have to do to be brilliant.

Did you know?

Your brain is not only the most complex organ in your body, it is the most intricate object in the universe. It's not much to look at: grey in colour, wrinkled like a walnut and with the texture of a wet sponge. Around 75 per cent water, your brain weighs around 1.5 kilograms; and, although that's only about 2 per cent of your bodyweight, it uses 20 per cent of the oxygen in your blood – carried in 100,000 miles of blood vessels. If you could harness its electrical power, the human brain could light up a 10-watt bulb.

Lose it, and still use it

People have lost large chunks of their brain and still been able to function, their mental systems shifting and sharing tasks and finding new ways to operate. Head injuries can have remarkably specific effects on thinking, showing that certain mental abilities are controlled by certain parts of the brain; but neuroscientists have found different bits of the same 'memory' in very different places, and modern imaging techniques reveal the complex interconnections involved in the simplest of tasks.

We've learnt much more about how the brain does specific things, but we're still at the very edge of understanding how its tangle of systems becomes memory – and, especially, *where* the memories are made and kept.

Mapping the memory

We think that memories are processed and stored all over the cerebral cortex, the brain's wrinkled outer layer. The four lobes specialise in particular aspects of memory: the frontal lobes, for example, play an important role in short-term learning and co-ordinating memories, drawing on the past and planning the future; and the temporal lobes major in autobiographical memory. And beneath the cortex, key parts of the brain appear to have their own roles to play.

- The *hippocampus* is heavily involved in transferring memories from short- to long-term storage and specialises in 'declarative' learning, the things you can talk about, and memory for shape and space. In a disease like Alzheimer's, the hippocampus is often the first area to be damaged, leading to confusion about details, spatial disorientation and a general inability to form new memories.

- The *cerebellum* is located at the back of the brain, near the spinal cord. This area is important for storing procedural memories and motor learning: skills involving good co-ordination and delicate control. These memories do tend to feel like they're stored in a different way from the rest: accessible without much conscious thought – and built to last.

- The *amygdala* has been shown to work with emotional memory, so if it's not operating properly you'll struggle to understand and process feelings. And emotions have a major impact on how memories are made and retrieved.

Memory is an extremely complex system. A lot has to happen for an experience to become a memory.

Short term/long term

Your brain is good at taking in information, but what happens next is less straightforward. We now think of 'short-term' memory as very short indeed. Your sense organs detect details, get them inside your head, and then the information is held on a very temporary basis in what's called 'working memory'. After that, *some* of it gets transferred to more lasting storage, 'long-term' memory – so training your memory involves learning to do four things well:

- gathering: using strong senses, concentrating and showing good attention to detail
- holding: having strategies for retaining information long enough to do something with it
- storing: taking ownership of the material, filing it effectively
- retrieving: knowing how to recover key bits of information, individually or in combination, for a variety of different needs

The vast amount of sense information you take in stays in your working memory just long enough to stand a chance of being remembered, thanks to some instinctive activities in the brain. Memory systems get to work to grasp hold of new material, beginning the process that will lead to *some* of it being stored for longer than the passing moment ... .

Holding sounds

Consider what happens when someone calls out their phone number to you. As you look for a pen and paper or your own phone, you're probably repeating the digits to yourself, either under your breath or in your imagination, keeping the fast-decaying information in your head for long enough to record it somewhere else. You're making use of your *phonological loop*.

Holding images

When you see a diagram or watch something moving you retain it as a picture in your head – for a while. This is your *visuo-spatial sketchpad* in action, and it also plays a role in planning movements. As someone gives you directions ('over the bridge, right at the traffic light, past the pub...') you're likely to create a mental picture and focus on it intently, trying to keep this imaginary map in front of your mind's eye.

Holding sequences

Your brain can integrate different sorts of information to form memorable sequences and structures, as words form into sentences, for example, or sights and sounds make up movie scenes. There's a limit, after which the sequence itself isn't enough, but up to that point you can remember 'the story so far' thanks to the natural power of the brain's *episodic buffer*.

All three of these systems are co-ordinated by the *central executive*, and together they provide you with the working memory that holds on to information in the short term. But there are some other important factors in play. Some things are simply easier for you to hold on to, and understanding *why* is a key early step towards boosting your brain.

ⓩ brilliant exercise

Throughout the history of memory testing, word lists have been used to investigate individuals' particular abilities, as well as to highlight common experiences and effects. To make the most of the following powerful experiment, try your best to switch off any active memory strategies and then ask someone to read the word list to you out loud. Just listen to the words and see which ones your brain retains without any conscious effort from you.

box   coat   oven   key   shark   pan   Elvis Presley   car   hole   whale laugh   pencil   sharpener   modern   octopus   hat   trophy   grey murder   rose   pin   starfish   book   firework   toast   seahorse   barrel fast   apple

If a computer was working properly, it wouldn't have any problem remembering these words. It could give them back to you forwards, backwards or in any other arrangement with 100 per cent accuracy, for ever. It wouldn't be put off by someone talking, get confused by previous word lists, be distracted between learning and recalling, lose energy or interest half way through ... Of course it might not find it so easy to tell you what it was doing on the day Elvis was shot, list its favourite makes of car or describe the wonders of the smell of toast, but it could be relied upon to return whatever you put in, efficiently and reliably.

Human memory is different, as you can demonstrate now by trying to write down all the words from the list that stuck in your mind – and then spending a moment thinking about what happened in your head during and after the test.

You may lose in a contest of simple recall, but you're instinctively doing more than just regurgitating the data as you spot subtle patterns, prioritise particular words, make connections, form images, personalise the information ... Your experience will be different from everyone else's, but there are also things in common that reflect some very important principles at work.

First and last

You're likely to remember words from the start of the list, like *box*, *coat* and *oven*. Your short-term memory had space, your brain was alert and you were interested in what was going to happen next. First impressions really do count: information gathered at the start of any learning exercise has a good chance of being recalled, thanks to what's called the *primacy effect*.

It's also easier to hold on to words from the end of the list. There may be 'interference' from the information that's come before, but there are no new words to overload your memory and not long to wait before you get the chance to answer. Your spirits tend to pick up towards the end of a learning session, adding to the power of the *recency effect*.

Surprise!

Information sticks more easily when it stands out in some way. It's another simple but incredibly powerful point. In this list, you were much more likely to remember the words *Elvis* and *Presley*: the only person – and a pretty outstanding one at that – amongst many mundane ideas. The next time you compose a shopping list, pick the two most important items, write them in larger letters using a different colour and style, and see if they're easier to remember. The *Von Restorff effect* says they will be. You could even add a completely inappropriate word somewhere in the list – *astronaut, banshee, Constantinople* – and see how quickly it comes to mind later on.

Sometimes, unusual information takes our attention from the other stuff and makes us remember less overall; but mostly, as advertisers, artists, comedians and the owners of brilliant memories know very well, details that stick out like a sore thumb stay *in* the mind longer than everything else.

Joined-up thinking

Connections are also incredibly powerful. In the list you saw, *pencil* and *sharpener* were clearly linked, as were all the sealife words: *shark, whale, octopus, starfish, seahorse.* Spotting patterns triggers memory and allows your brain to cluster the individual bits together, and 'chunking' is a well-known memory tactic: grouping information into more manageable bundles. So *12, 24, 10, 16* isn't really any harder to hold in the mind than *2, 4, 0, 6,* and *shoe, cake, banana, tree, elephant* is as easy at *s, c, b, t, e.* Your brain does it naturally all the time, but you can also start to do it consciously: learning guest-list names in pairs, for example, or organising your Christmas buying list into 'themed' groups of gifts.

Think about the other words you remembered. Some will probably be easy to picture, like *trophy* or *firework.* Others will evoke senses – *toast* – inspire an emotional reaction – *murder* – or simply catch your attention in some other way, perhaps connecting to something you're doing today or prompting you to notice an item nearby.

Eminently forgettable

And the words you're *least* likely to remember? They're the ones in the middle of the list, with nothing to make them stand out, no connections with other words, hard to picture, uninspiring, abstract … And how well that describes so much of the information you struggle to remember in real life! No wonder so many things never get any further than your short-term memory.

There were other tricky aspects of this learning task, more factors that a computer wouldn't have to worry about – like anxiety about failing, having little real motivation to succeed, only hearing the information once … And, once again, how often are these things true of your day-to-day memory attempts?

Left to its own devices, your memory will remember some things, forget others, follow typical patterns, behave inconsistently and inefficiently, surprise you, frustrate you ... *but it doesn't have to be that way.* Now that you've spotted the key things that help and hinder memory, you can start putting the right conditions in place to achieve a much better level of success. This is your chance to make the most of your brain's complex characteristics, its connectedness and creativity. This is where you start to outperform the computer, using memory skills to explore information imaginatively and to apply it in ingenious ways. And all the while you're developing core aspects of your thinking that will help you do *everything* better.

This is where you start to take control.

Get organised

Far too often we struggle to remember information in its most forgettable form. A computer can either cope with a particular format or it can't, and tells you so; but most of the time we just push on and try to make material stick, however badly it's presented. Our brain does its best to break the task into manageable chunks and to find useable patterns – but having a brilliant memory involves a much more conscious approach. Like the ancient masters of the art of memory, you find a new design for your data: one that matches the way your brain works best.

Matchmaking

Even simple attempts at organisation can make a big difference. Suddenly the puzzle has fewer pieces, and it can even start to feel like it's solving itself, giving clues about what goes where. You can see this in action by re-reading the word list as a set of fifteen pairs rather than thirty individual ideas. Spend a few moments now looking through the information – basically, the same list – in this new form, thinking about each pair as a single item. Even without much effort you'll find that your brain is picturing the two words combined in some way or spotting something that links them.

box, coat   oven, key   shark, pan   Elvis, Presley   car, hole
whale, laugh   pencil, sharpener   modern, octopus
hat, trophy   grey, murder   rose, pin   starfish, book
firework, toast   seahorse, barrel   fast, apple

It should already feel easier. You've instantly halved the items and given your brain some much more memorable ideas: a 'car hole', a 'whale laugh', some 'firework toast' … Combining concepts like this also stops them being mundane and kick-starts your imagination, giving these fifteen items a much greater chance of staying put.

True, you've now looked through the list a second time – but in real life, re-reading information doesn't always make much of a difference. This time, see whether it's had any impact on your learning. How many of the thirty words can you remember now?

And to get a feel for the 'glue' your brain can use to hold the pieces together, see if you can remember what came after each of the words below.

box _____   fast _____   modern _____
whale _____   oven _____   grey _____
rose _____   firework _____   Elvis _____
shark _____   starfish _____   pencil _____
car _____   hat _____   seahorse _____

There's an active approach at work here, since you've carefully reorganised the original list; but it's also about *allowing* your brain to do what comes naturally. We're wired to ask questions, look for patterns, try to survive by working out what's going on – so throwing together unconnected items wakes up the brain and challenges it to make meaning. Normally you might not concentrate much on words like *pan, toast* or *laugh,* but now it's hard *not* to imagine what a 'shark pan' might look like, a 'whale laugh' sound like, or what smell might emerge from some 'firework toast'.

Storytelling

When you give it a chance, your brain loves to tell stories, finding some sort of logic to structure separate pieces of information. There's a natural instinct to 'put two and two together' – and, in memory terms, when it does make five, that's even better! Unusual outcomes are the ones that stick in the mind, as long as there's some degree of method in the madness.

Oral storytelling helped us to keep hold of our shared history long before anything was written down. These days we have countless storytelling formats: poems, songs, novels, movies, adverts, anecdotes, instructions, video-games …

Throughout this book you'll see the power of stories to make anything memorable.

So, if you're sitting comfortably, here's a story about …

… a huge box packed with expensive fur coats. In the pocket of one of the coats you find an oven key, and when you use it to unlock a secret compartment in your oven you discover something unusual inside: a shark pan, full of great white sharks. One of the sharks is chasing Elvis Presley, but he manages to crawl through a car hole and escape, dodging all the cars that are also coming in and out through the hole. Just when Elvis thinks he's free, he hears the deep, booming sound of a whale laugh, so he hides behind a giant pencil sharpener – where he meets a very modern octopus who's also in hiding. In each one of the octopus' eight tentacles is a hat trophy, its prizes for winning a hat-making competition. Elvis looks carefully at one of the hat-shaped trophies and sees a strange image on it: a

grey photograph of a gruesome crime scene. He peels off this 'grey murder' and uses a rose-shaped pin to fix it to the starfish book he's carrying, pressing the flowery pin right through one of the beautiful starfish illustrations. But this makes the book explode, shooting fireworks made out of toast into the night sky, each firework showering the crowds below with toast crumbs. Someone decides to catch the crumbs in a seahorse barrel, and the seahorses inside start to eat them noisily, until a fast apple starts darting around the barrel and getting to the crumbs first ...

It's a strange story. There's no logic involved in firework toast falling into seahorse barrels and being snatched by fast apples ... but there is a clear set of connections at work, an explicable if decidedly odd chain of events, reminiscent of dreams. And if the images and ideas are strong and memorable enough, you should be able to follow them from start to finish – and rediscover the original thirty words along the way.

Remembering ...

Put it to the test. Start by looking into the huge box, see what you find – and where the story takes you. How many of the thirty words do you know now, and how well can you remember the order?

See what happens when you try to recall the list backwards. The apple was fast in the barrel full of seahorses, catching toast from ... what? Can you make it all the way back to the start of the story?

And what about answering specific questions about the details in between?

- What came after *sharpener*?
- What was the eighth word on the list?
- Which word came before *toast*?

- Which of these words was not on the original list: *hat, oven, candle, modern*?
- How many of the words ended in a vowel?

Remembering like this may seem silly to start with, but it *works*, allowing you to perform precise, controlled feats of recall. Suddenly, instead of just being thankful for whatever your brain happens to hold on to, you're taking active control – and reaping the rewards. You strengthen your concentration, kick-start your creativity, and develop a range of key thinking skills that will serve you well in many different tasks. And, above all, you get a glimpse of what it might feel like to be able to remember anything. If you can learn a list of thirty random words, backwards, forwards and inside out, what else might you be able to do?

... and forgetting

So would you remember the list tomorrow, next week, in ten years from now? Unlike a computer, your brain can perform brilliantly in a task like this one minute, then really struggle the next. While you're focused and motivated, and the memorable images and links are fresh in your mind, an amazing feat of recall is possible, and there's no reason why you couldn't practise every day, repeat the same learning activity regularly and keep remembering this list for decades to come. But if you didn't, the memories would almost certainly fade. Sometimes life can feel like a constant battle to hold on to information as it slips away like sand through your fingers.

And yet ... some memories are there for the long haul. Some information goes through the whole memory process, starting as sensory inputs, being held in working memory and short-term storage, then getting filed in a much more long-lasting way, with no further need for repetition and rehearsal. Enough has been done to it to achieve something close to permanence.

I'll always remember ...

A sound or a smell takes you back thirty years to a memory that's still as clear as if it happened yesterday. Your daughter's name is on your lips without a second's pause for thought. At the pub quiz, some bits of information pop out of nowhere, learnt long ago and just waiting for the right moment. And you know what they say about learning to ride a bike ...

Of course, illness or accident can still cause problems, and everyone makes the odd mistake. Health and mood, time and place, distractions and diversions: there are many factors that can play havoc with even the most secure memories. But what's clear is that your brain can take some information and make it truly memorable. And when you understand *how*, you're another step closer to putting your memory under your control.

It's a simple idea, but a life-changing one. When you know what's involved in making lasting memories – and you're about to – you can start doing it whenever you want.

 brilliant recap

- Training your core thinking skills is a vital part of boosting your memory.
- Memory is a complex set of systems involving many parts of the brain.
- There are clear patterns to remembering and forgetting in practice.
- Short-term memory is *very* short, but the crucial first step to learning anything.
- Memory techniques make the most of the way your brain works best.

CHAPTER 4

Taking control

When I was younger, I could
remember anything, whether it
had happened or not.

Mark Twain

In this chapter you will learn:

- why some information gets stored in long-term memory
- how your brain remembers different things in different ways
- the seven steps to putting memory under your control
- ways to manage your emotions and stay focused on learning
- techniques for using your creative imagination to revolutionise your memory

For many people, unless an experience is so powerful that it burns itself into their brain, the only way of transferring information from short-term to long-term memory is to practise. Repetition certainly has an important role to play in learning, and the things we remember regularly do gain a special place in our minds. But there's much more to memory than that. More has to happen for lasting memories to be made. And even when that's happened – and even with those moments you know you'll never forget – repeat remembering is a complex process in which the original information doesn't stay original for long. It gets changed as the brain's natural creativity takes over. The details are altered as they're enriched and absorbed into the brain's interconnected storage systems – and, for good or bad, that's how the strongest memories are made.

This chapter gives you a step-by-step guide to the whole memory process, revealing what you can do to take more control. You need to be aware of what your brain does naturally, and make the most of it; but there are also some very practical actions you can take to do things differently and remember *much* more.

⟁ brilliant exercise

Without looking at your wristwatch, cover it up. (And if you don't wear a watch, do the same thing with your mobile phone or some other item that you look at many times during the day.) Now try to describe your watch from memory. Exactly what shape is the face, what colour is the strap, what sort of fastener holds it on your wrist? Are there numbers or Roman numerals? Is there any writing visible? What other distinctive details can you remember? When you've remembered everything you can, have a look at your watch to see how well you did. Most people are very surprised at how weak their memory is for something they've seen thousands of times. Clearly repetition isn't enough to make memories, especially detailed memories – even though it's many people's learning technique of choice.

So for some types of remembering the process needs to be more than just repetition if it's going to work. And yet we are creatures of habit: we do repeat certain behaviours and rehearse particular memories. Practice can certainly fix things in our brains – and not always to our benefit.

Ever-changing memories

Practice plays more of a part in memory than you might think. That vivid moment from your childhood, the embarrassing episode at work last year, even a first date two days ago that you've been remembering repeatedly ever since: how much has practice actually altered the information? You've strengthened the basic space it occupies in your memory, but how many of the details have changed, every time you remembered the last time you remembered …? Has practice embedded memories that are now very different from the original things they recall?

Practice helps to forge strong memories, but it's more than just doing the same things again and again. It's about enriching, adding, strengthening, and *changing* information in the process, to make it stand the test of time.

What's so powerful about the *Brilliant Memory Training* approach to learning is that it *begs* to be enriched. It's not like the hours you might have spent reading and re-reading revision notes, or the number of times you looked through the same presentation script without any more of it going in. That sort of memory felt like starting from scratch every time. *This* sort is about making the most of every bit of practice, strengthening the mental connections and using the way your brain works to build memories that last.

Conscious creativity

To have a brilliant memory you need to recognise the creativity involved in many aspects of your natural memory processes, then use it to your advantage. Your brain is already very good at picking out some things to remember, creating strong images, developing and exaggerating them repeatedly and embedding memories that are intensely personal versions of the original information – just not always the things you want to learn.

But under your control your mind can focus on whatever you want and start to remember it brilliantly. You've seen what's going on when your brain works well, and that knowledge is vital as you start giving your chosen information the 'memorability' it needs.

You've glimpsed what your memory can do when you start using it differently. Now it's time to take charge of what goes in and *stays* in.

Survival skills

To survive we've always needed to prioritise. Your brain is built to focus on the things that are likely to have the greatest impact on your survival and success; but it's overprotective, and the pictures it produces can be wildly inaccurate. Hear about a plane crash on the car-radio, for example, and the story is likely to skew your perception of danger and make you forget that you're at much greater risk right there in your car. As a child, if you're scared by something specific, like a neighbour's dog or a burst balloon, your brain is very good at filing powerful reminders to help you avoid those feelings in the future, but they're not always proportionate to the real risks at hand. This is how many phobias begin: an unpleasant moment exaggerated and fixed in the memory long after it's served any protective purpose.

In memory terms it's an absolutely vital concept to understand. With a little training you can start using this innate ability to make things 'big', *choosing* the things you want to be significant instead of just letting them slip by unnoticed. Giving information significance is at the heart of memory training, and it happens in your infinite imagination.

When need just isn't enough

A learning task itself can be significant if it might make you money, win you promotion, impress your friends – or avoid the shame of failing an exam or having to retake your driving test. But even then, as anyone who's struggled to learn for a high-stakes exam knows only too well, if the information you need to remember doesn't have the right level of importance – is abstract, boring and flat – no amount of personal motivation seems to help. In fact, when the level of urgency is so different from the level of 'memorability', that's when complete brain-freeze can strike.

Significance

As well as a certain degree of commitment to the challenge, to get you concentrating and learning actively, the material itself needs to hold 'significance' if your brain is going to prioritise it and take it in. That significance comes in four key forms: *connection*, *visibility*, *exaggeration* and *difference*.

Connection

It's easier to remember things that are about you. Being interested in the information is a good first step, but it's even better if stronger emotions are aroused, connecting you through real excitement, surprise, fear, delight, attraction, disappointment, embarrassment, ecstasy.

Visibility

It makes a huge difference to your memory whether or not you can see the information you need to learn, and how much detail and colour and richness it has to offer. The power of images was recognised very early in the history of memory improvement, but we still struggle to learn material in the least visible form possible: black and white words on a page; or, worse, abstract ideas heard, not even written down, offering no images at all to help. Young children use books packed with memorable pictures, but as adults we often work without any visual aids, handicapping our memory from the word go.

Exaggeration

The advertising industry knows how to create memorable images. Think about the adverts – on TV, at the cinema, in newspapers and on billboards – that stand out in your mind. Even on the radio it's possible to use music, sound effects and creative ideas to build particularly strong images.

The most powerful pictures are exaggerated in some way: huge or tiny, colourful, fast-moving, loud, dazzling, extremely ... *something*. In your imagination, absolutely anything is possible – just like in the world of cartoons or fairytales – so it makes sense to do everything you can to heighten your imagery: to make it unforgettable.

Difference

The most memorable information is outstanding: in its own right, but it also tends to be very different from everything else. When you review your day-to-day experiences, it's the unusual moments that stand out. If they were *all* wedding days or competition wins or first births, they'd quickly lose their special power as they blended into one. To stay memorable, your images need to be special and distinct – and this will become increasingly important as you set your targets higher and start accumulating large amounts of information. An important feature of brilliant memory is the flexibility of thought that allows you to create strikingly original ideas.

brilliant tip

It's your turn to buy the drinks at the bar and there are lots of very similar orders: white wine, red wine, orange-juice, beer, white wine, beer, orange-juice, white wine, beer ... You could easily imagine a huge white grape balanced on top of Jamie's head to remind you of his drink, but you'd have to do something different for Emma, who also wants white wine: so how about imagining her pouring a bottle of wine on to her black dress and watching it turn bright white? Sam and Claudia both want orange-juice, so you'll have to make their reminder pictures distinct. How about one of them juggling oranges wildly, and the other one pulling on a huge orange hat?

Memories for everything

So memory boosting involves changing information to make it compatible with the in-built mannerisms and mechanisms of your brain. Some learning challenges are harder than others, and there are times when your memory really has very little chance of working: those rushed, one-chance moments when the information is distant and abstract and mundane and similar. There are also particular types of memory that need special attention.

Prospective memory

This is remembering things that haven't even happened yet. You know you need to call the school or go to the bank on the way home or buy your mother-in-law's birthday present, but there's no experience yet to form a strong memory, and even important jobs can be easily forgotten. This book will show you how to create powerful images for future events, using all the key creative skills to embed these 'memories of the future'.

Procedural memory

This involves knowing how to do things. It can feel easy when it's embedded and practised, but getting to that stage can be a big challenge. A lot depends on the quality of your teacher or manual, how quickly you get to try things out and how long you have to practise; but crucial once again is your ability to take control of all the information coming your way. These days, learning new skills – and coping when old processes change – is one of the most important tests of your memory. The training you've started will show you how to hold instructions long enough to change them, and then to do so quickly and powerfully, to *make* them memorable.

Semantic memory

This is your knowledge of the world. Again, when it works, it's easy to take for granted the store of facts and figures and core understanding you've built up. But adding to that store can be a problem, especially when the stakes are high and the information doesn't immediately excite your imagination and activate your memory. Revising for exams, preparing for a big presentation, remembering names at a conference, learning enough of a new language to cope on your travels: even with all the information in front of you and plenty of time to study, learning can be frustrating and stressful – and, when put to the test, just not work very well – unless you know how.

Episodic memory

This kind of memory can seem very easy. It's your recall of events and experiences, including the most personal ones – *autobiographical memory* – and many moments do stick in your mind without any noticeable effort: but not all of them. Like anything else they need to have certain characteristics if they're likely to stay there in the long term. The strategies you're developing will help you to remember new experiences in greater detail, and to explore moments from the past – especially *your* past – in different and exciting ways. But most important of all, you'll be using your natural flair with this kind of memory to boost all the others; because *anything* can be turned into a powerful experience in your imagination and remembered with as much clarity as the real things you've been through.

Child's play

Give a child a stick, tell them it's a horse, a sword or a witch's broom, and they can immediately transform it in their imagination and play with their new toy for hours. As adults we still use our imaginative skills regularly, reading books, watching plays, designing, planning, worrying … but we're likely to feel much less confident at taking the lead and *applying* imagination to the situations we face. But there's no reason why we can't start using it again, to have fun, experiment, practise, and learn in a very efficient and effective way; although some adults find it comes much more naturally than others ...

🔍 brilliant exercise

The following task shows you this powerful approach in action. It's another list of words to learn – random information which could just as easily be ideas for a presentation, presents to buy on a busy shopping trip or key vocabulary in a new foreign language. It's important to prove that you can train yourself to remember anything – and this exercise will also reveal the seven key steps involved in doing it brilliantly.

bag   angel   sausage   painting   field   rocket   sand   river   spoon
eye   cat   squeeze   Hawaii   queen   dance   socks   snake   car
lighthouse   tomato

Step 1: Deciding
You're going to learn all twenty words, forwards, backwards and inside out. You'll be putting your creative brain in control, changing this information until it sits comfortably in your memory and can be kept there for as long as you want. You'll impress yourself, boost your confidence, learn more about your memory and start getting into the habit of remembering anything.

Step 2: Strategising
Rather than simply reading the words and hoping that they stick, you're about to turn them into an unforgettable story, with you at the centre. You'll invent powerful image clues for every word, link them into a strong chain, and make sure that every detail has maximum impact. You're going to invest the time it takes to create a new version of this material that will be enriched every time you think about it and provide you with a robust and reliable long-term memory store.

Step 3: Visualising

Each word needs to be given a clear image, and that's easier for some of them than others. You could think about:

- how an artist might illustrate this word
- the image you'd choose to represent it on a presentation slide
- the costume you'd wear if it was the theme for a fancy-dress party

Push yourself to 'see' each image in your mind's eye and check it's a good clue for the word in question. These pictures themselves won't store all the information for you, but they're already boosting your memory and giving your brain the starting-points it needs.

Step 4: Personalising

You're going to turn a set of images into a memorable story, and the most memorable stories are about you. Start noticing any words that have particular relevance for you: favourites, pet-hates, interests. Which words spark existing memories that you could use? Which senses and emotions come to mind as you look at the list?

Step 5: Exaggerating

How can you make each image special in some way, so that it stands out and sticks powerfully in your memory?

This step is a crucial checkpoint in the process because it ensures that you're studying details, visualising clearly, personalising where possible, and doing everything you can to *make* the information memorable.

Step 6: Organising

You're going to create a clear and organised structure for your images, helping to hold them in your memory and giving you flexible access to the information they represent. The organising technique in this case will be a story: a chain of events that links each word to the next. You'll need to think carefully about the most memorable ways to connect the images so that each one triggers the next. If your organising structure is good enough, it will let you recall the words backwards as well as forwards, start at any point in the pattern, and identify individual words from anywhere on the list.

Step 7: Practising

Finally, you're going to practise – but not in the traditional sense of reading your material repeatedly or chanting it until it becomes automatic. Carefully crafted images and clear connections will fix the information in your mind at the first time of asking, so that rehearsing them just enriches and strengthens the memories further. Every time you bring the story to mind, your imagination will subtly change the images and links, adding new layers of detail and useful memory triggers. The act of remembering will be enjoyable and rich, and *that's* what you'll remember the next time you do it.

So, after deciding to do it, working out your approach and having some ideas about how to create personal, powerful, patterned images ... it's time to create the imaginative story that will prove just how brilliant your memory can be.

Everybody's story will be different – and *needs* to be, to make it powerfully personal – but here's one version that demonstrates many of the key imaginative techniques. Use it to practise this new way of thinking, but feel free to change any of the images and links, to add your own associations, and to see it all very much from your perspective. That's how you'll take control of it all in *your* mind.

Imagine ... (really imagine, really picture these images and events, really bring them to life in your head) ...

… opening your beautiful and very expensive new leather bag and seeing an angel climb out, glowing and shimmering in a bright white gown with a shining halo around her head. The angel is carrying something: look closely at her hand and you'll see that she's clutching a sausage, which you can smell from here. You'd love to have a taste, but before you can get anywhere near, the angel hurls the sausage across the room, hitting a priceless painting hanging on the wall: splat. *And it must have hit hard because the painting falls, sliding down the wall and hitting the floor, the glass smashing into millions of pieces. But there's no time to tidy up because the accident has revealed something: a hole in the wall behind the painting, through which you can see a field. It's green and calm and smells of fresh air, but something's about to happen that will shatter the serenity. A rocket is sitting on the launchpad in the middle of the field, and suddenly it takes off, exploding into the air with a mighty roar and almost blinding you with its fiery exhaust. You watch it rise high above your head, but you can feel something showering down from on high: sand. Golden sand is leaking from the rocket, a long trail of it dropping to earth where it starts to cover everything. This is worrying: it's falling into rivers and quickly blocking their flow. You know you've got to do something, but all you've got with you is a spoon, and although you try to use your spoon to dig out the sand, you don't get very far – especially when you accidentally flick sand in your eye. Suddenly everything's black, you can't see a thing. You stumble backwards – but luckily you feel something warm and soft behind you. As your vision comes back, you look round to see that you've sunk into the soft, furry lap of a huge cat, surely the biggest cat in the world, sitting there and purring contentedly. It's a lovely feeling … until the cat starts to squeeze you. It squeezes harder and harder until you're struggling to breathe. Although you fight it, you lose consciousness: and the next thing you know …* you're lying on an island. The obvious question is, where are you? *There are plenty of clues around: hot weather, the ocean, girls in grass skirts, long canoes, even the theme-tune to* Hawaii Five-O *playing somewhere in the distance. You're on a beach in Hawaii – and look, here comes*

the queen, processing towards you with her servants in tow. You're nervous about what to say to royalty, but she doesn't want to talk: she wants to dance, *grabbing your hands and whirling you round in a long and complicated dance. You move so quickly that one of your socks – your favourite pink ones – flies off. You try to grab it; but, just as your hand touches the sock, a snake slithers out, hissing menacingly in your direction. Everyone screams, everyone runs, and luckily there's a car parked nearby and you jump inside and drive away – but smash straight into a lighthouse. You get out to inspect the damage. The car's a write-off, and the tall lighthouse is now leaning and wobbling, its beams of light flickering and then cutting out altogether as the lighthouse topples to the ground. All you can do is stand and watch as it falls on top of someone's giant, prize-winning tomato. Red juice squirts everywhere and you feel it running down your face. You taste a bit: sweet and delicious.*

The story looks long on paper, but every detail has been written out and all the links made explicit. With a bit of practice you'll be able to tell a memorable story like this in not much more time than it takes to read the list itself. The images will come quickly and the events unfold naturally – and of course everything will automatically be easier when you're inventing the ideas for yourself.

brilliant tip

It's a very common reaction to think: 'But now there's more to remember. What if I can't remember the story?' You *will* remember the story because it's been written that way. Everything in it is designed to *help* you remember, to suit the way your brain works best. There's a range of multi-sensory reminders, a clear chain of events, questions along the way to get you predicting what's next, details added to be interesting, surprising, funny, scary … so just let your brain pick up on the clues and trust that you're going to find remembering easy.

The memory story began when you opened a bag and found something unusual inside. Go through the weird and wonderful events that came next, thinking carefully about the twenty key images and what each of them represents. Try to remember all twenty words in exactly the right order. When you've had a go at that, can you also do it backwards?

What came after *field*? What was the word between *angel* and *painting*? What was the seventeenth word on the list? Which of the following words was not amongst the original words: *cat*, *cone*, *queen*, *spoon*?

Can you feel your memory being stretched and strengthened?

🔎 brilliant exercise

It's important that you try this approach for yourself as soon as possible. You're still in the early stages of your memory training, so don't worry if this way of thinking feels awkward or a bit too much like hard work. Trust me, if you start putting in the effort now, you'll soon be doing it instinctively and reaping the rewards. You may actually be pleasantly surprised by how much you can do already, using the skills and strategies you've learnt so far.

Here's your next list. Follow all the steps you've been shown to take control of the information and change it into pictures and links that your brain will find hard to forget.

sheep   cheese   paint   windmill   weight   computer   December
happy   carpet   love   clown   basketball   pyjamas   radio   chicken
rain   spider   monopoly   pizza   dragon

Spend a moment practising your story, focusing on each of the key features and confirming the clues and the links, then cover the list and say the words from memory, forwards, backwards, every other word … Pick a word at random and see how quickly you can say what came immediately before and after. How many words on the list begin with consonants? What was the twelfth word?

Notice how it feels to use your brain like this. Enjoy every success you achieve, but also make a note of any difficulties you encounter. The next chapter will help you to fix problems, honing all the skills involved in getting the best out of your brain and unleashing your full memory power.

brilliant recap

- Repetition doesn't guarantee remembering.

- You remember your experiences creatively – and that can be very useful.

- There are seven essential steps to remembering brilliantly.

- Your imagination can make any kind of information powerfully memorable.

- Recall more by being relaxed and positive, and learning from your mistakes.

CHAPTER 5

Global learning

No brain is stronger than its weakest think.

Thomas L. Masson

In this chapter you will learn:

- that there are two sides to your brain, with their own attributes and abilities
- how to harness both hemispheres to get the most out of your memory
- practical techniques for boosting your imagination
- the power of senses to enrich memory
- new ideas about organising information to make it stick

Your brain is capable of the most incredible things, but you need to know how to tap all its resources and enjoy its full capacity for brilliance. Too many people struggle on much less than full power.

It's easy to feel that your memory isn't up to the task. When you're rushed, tired, stressed, over-worked, multi-tasking ... when information is presented in unmemorable ways ... when you just can't find the time, space, energy or motivation to take any kind of active control ... it's tempting to think that this is it: this is the way your memory has to feel. True, there are many things that can get in the way, but don't give up, don't automatically fall back on habits that aren't working. The best memory strategies are actually incredibly simple, designed to match the way your brain has been built. And often it only takes a slight shift to get your thinking skills in gear and working brilliantly.

We've complained about bad memories for centuries, even though there have been plenty of people keen to show us the light. Back in the 1600s, the multi-talented English writer, historian, churchman and philosopher Thomas Fuller explained that memory *'depends very much on the perspicuity, regularity, and order of our thoughts. Many complain of the want of memory, when the defect is in the judgement; and others, by grasping at all, retain nothing.'* He knew that our attempts at learning will always be fallible and frustrating unless we use our brains properly.

Imagination …

Thomas Fuller called it 'perspicuity', and you certainly need imaginative clarity to have a brilliant memory. Chapter 3 got you designing and manipulating images to represent key pieces of information, and you've already experienced the power of your creative brain. In this chapter you'll be strengthening all the skills involved in imagining the richest, most detailed, most memorable pictures as you discover how to get more out of your creative thinking.

… and order

You'll also learn more about what Fuller called 'regularity' and 'order', exploring new techniques for organising information in your memory. Just as the best memory techniques promote creativity in general, they can also boost your ability to organise your thinking and structure your approach to life – which, like creativity, feeds back into your memory.

And when these two key aspects of thinking come together, a bit of Fuller's 'judgement' will let you apply your brilliant memory to a wide range of practical tasks, real scenarios and personal challenges. All the techniques in this book are based on a powerful combination of these two types of thinking: imagination and logic. To understand why, and to see how this really is the secret of your success, you need to spend a few minutes looking inside your head.

Both sides now

Look at a human brain and it has two clear hemispheres, left and right. You'll have seen 'phrenology' models that cover these hemispheres with labels, suggesting that particular areas are responsible for things like 'language', 'affection' or 'memory of people', and no doubt you've also heard about 'right-brained' and 'left-brained' thinking – the idea that mental processes are grouped on either side to give the hemispheres distinct characteristics. For around two hundred years now, neuroscientists have been trying to map the geography of the brain, aiming to localise particular functions and to define the workings of the two hemispheres, separately and in combination. Important discoveries have been made; but, despite temptingly neat phrenology maps and all those right brain/left brain tests you can take, the emerging picture is a very complex one. The good news is that it contains some essential information about improving your memory.

Broken minds

There are some useful clues in early research on damaged brains. In the 1860s, two influential scientists, Pierre Paul Broca and Carl Wernicke, found locations in the left brain responsible for particular functions of language, meaning that patients had very clear deficits when those sites weren't working. But they also demonstrated that a skill as complex as 'language' is distributed to different areas; and, significantly, that the 'logical' bits, like vocabulary and grammar, seemed to be controlled by the left side, while more subtle, creative skills like pronunciation and reading of context were associated with the right. That left brain/right brain contrast would become a key theme in thinking-about-thinking in the years to come.

In the 1940s, Wilder Penfield's open-brain experiments demonstrated that the left and right brains have different motor functions, the left controlling the right side of the body and vice versa. He was also able to map how the brain handles particular senses; but although some of his work emphasised localised thinking, his biggest discovery was about the interconnectedness of the brain – especially regarding the making and storing of memories. When his patients had particular parts of their brains stimulated with electrodes – while they were conscious and communicative – they reported incredibly realistic memories of moments from their lives, rich in all the senses at once. It seemed the memories had been made that way, packed with information drawn from different sense centres across the brain. Initially, Penfield saw this as evidence that memories were stored in specific physical sites, but his later research suggested that those sites were more like 'access points', and that memories were distributed much more widely, stored somehow by the *whole* brain.

This was backed up by Karl Lashley's experiments with rats. He found that they could still remember their way through mazes even when significant parts of their brain had been removed. Karl Pribram, a student of Penfield's, noticed that his patients didn't lose particular memories when large parts of their brain were gone, they just developed hazier pictures of the past. And when he read an article about holograms, he realised that science had come up with a very powerful analogy for memory.

brilliant definition

The holographic brain

A hologram is one of those 3D photographs created by laser on a glass plate: a 'virtual image' that seems to exist before your eyes but has no substance when you reach out to touch it. For the memory researchers, a crucial aspect of holograms is that, when they're smashed into pieces, each individual bit still holds the original image, just with a weaker resolution. The information is stored somewhere and everywhere, the virtual image constructed from the pieces but not just any one piece, and not necessarily all of them … The holographic brain model has had a huge influence on the way we've thought about memory in the decades since.

Split thinking

But while the whole brain seems to help with managing your memory, your two cerebral hemispheres do have particular roles to play in the way you think. In the 1960s, Roger Sperry and his team in the USA revealed a number of processes clearly specialised in either side of the brain, defining the 'character' of each hemisphere; but, once again, their research also showed that our two brains are designed to work together, and follow-up studies have revealed more about the overlap between left and right – more capacity for the brain to do anything *anywhere*.

Matching the early findings of men like Broca and Wernicke, Sperry showed that the left brain is dominant in logical thinking, while the right is biased towards creativity.

Left versus right

The left brain is good at analysing, organising and defining. In terms of language, this means remembering the definitions of words and the structures of grammar and syntax. In maths, it's exact calculation and precise comparison.

The right brain excels in responding to language, emotional reactions, subjective judgements. Its mathematical skills are approximation and finding more general patterns.

So clearly you need both sides to be working well. The left brain manages the details but you're lost without the right brain's vision of the bigger picture. If your right brain recognises faces, you need your left brain to help you with the names. Left-brained computation and reasoning need to be backed up by right-brained understanding and intuition. Skills like music, poetry and visual art may be more right-brained in nature, but they're all underpinned by left-brained thinking.

Excuses, excuses

Although it should have demonstrated the powerful, interconnected brilliance of the brain, the left brain/right brain theory has had some rather negative results. Quickly people started labelling themselves as 'left-brained' or 'right-brained' and using that label as an excuse for difficulties rather than as an incentive to improve. Thinking styles were separated – scorned, sometimes: 'She's far too right-brained to get the finer points'; 'Luckily I'm a right-brainer and I know how to have fun'.

Our individual characters certainly make us more inclined to different types of thinking, and we'll find some things harder than others. But the goal for everyone should be to achieve '*both-brained*' status, able to use either side when necessary but always to get the most out of both. Bringing them together is what brings real success, especially when you want to get more out of your memory.

Whole-brain memory

You needed to glimpse some of the science in order to under-stand the memory techniques you're developing in this book. It's really important to realise that all the best strategies and systems have been designed to suit the way the brain works – and that, yes, your brain is perfectly capable of putting them into practice.

It's no coincidence that every effective memory method brings together both sides of the brain. You design powerful pictures, add rich layers of senses and emotions, have fun, take risks, use your right-brained creativity to the full ... but you also organise your imagery, give it structure, connect it together, learn strate-gically, and use left-brained logic to complete the task.

When it comes to recalling what you learnt, you have left-brain access to the details and can analyse, calculate and compare. And ... you can explore it all with engagement and emotion, and see the potential power of the *whole*.

Then and now

The right and left sides of your thinking also relate to different times in your life. Spend a moment considering how your learning skills have changed over the years, the pros and cons of different stages of memory maturity, and you'll realise that whole-brained thinking requires all of you.

When you were a child you learned fearlessly. You explored the world through all your senses, shaking, biting, smelling. Learning was active, adventurous and fun. Your books were full of colourful pictures. You played while you worked, with physical toys but also in the limitless world of your imagina-tion. Your teachers used stories and games to activate your memory. Some things, like languages, were learnt in a richly contextual way that would never be possible again. And yet ... your memory was also very hit-and-miss. Children's memories can easily be manipulated, and you only have to look in the lost-property box in school to realise how often children forget. As a child you had easy access to many of the most important right-brained modes of thought, but lacked some key thinking tools from the left.

Adults are more competent at logical, left-brained thinking. They have responsibilities, priorities. The success or failure of their work has big implications. The grown-up you can certainly still enjoy learning through play, exploring with your senses and investigating in your imagination. But life is very different now. Your learning materials tend to have far fewer pictures. Information comes at you in a much less prettified and patterned form. Rather than building up your understanding in context, step by step, you're often called upon to process ideas piecemeal and to handle abstract bits of data. You do have the ability to be strategic, though, to prioritise tasks and set up systems to give your memory the best chance of success. You juggle information more efficiently, multi-skill and balance long- and short-term tasks. Your left brain is well-used now, but what's happened to the rich resources of the right?

Kick-start your imagination

You may think you have a poor imagination, but you're probably showing it off every day – and *night,* in your creative, surreal, richly imaginative dreams. As adults we're constantly challenged to find imaginative solutions to problems. We visualise scenarios when we're chatting at the water-cooler. We manipulate imagery as we talk through complex issues on the phone. We bring audio-books and radio plays to life in our imagination, lose ourselves in books, movies and video-games … But what we're not so good at is switching on our imagination consciously when it comes to learning, especially when the material in question seems to cry out for logical, left-brained thought.

The following exercises will help to train your visual imagination as well as strengthening all the other senses you could use. The more sense connections you include, the more vivid and accessible your memories will be.

Sight

You've got eight jobs to remember, and you're going to create a clear mental picture for each one.

- Go to the bank.
- Pick up the dry cleaning.
- Book an appointment with your child's teacher.
- Buy flowers.
- Get petrol.
- Send a birthday card to Scott.
- Return the library books.
- Pay the vet's bill.

Go to the bank

What would be a strong image to remind you of the first job on the list? Perhaps a security van full of money, the heavily guarded underground vault or the bank teller's window. Choose your picture, then spend a moment focusing on it in your mind.

brilliant timesaver

To begin with, trust your instincts and accept the first picture your brain throws up. You have a vast store of representative images, so it makes sense and saves time to start from something that's already there. There'll be plenty of occasions when you do need to put your creative imagination to the test, inventing images for complex or abstract ideas; but, when the information is familiar, go straight to a familiar version of it in your memory.

View your picture from one direction and think about its overall shape. Make sure you've captured the image as a whole, but then take a closer look at its colours, shapes-within-shapes, writing, unusual features ... Finally, practise seeing it from different perspectives. Imagine getting close up and far away, inside, round the back, underneath, high above. You're used to using your imagination to think through practical problems from different angles, but it can take a bit of training to switch it on like this and start using your visualisation skills to the full.

Pick up dry cleaning
You could create an image of the inside of the dry cleaner's itself, a bag of newly cleaned clothes, or anything else that would represent this task in your mind. Again, get the basic picture sorted first, then add more and more visual details. Use 'extreme close-ups' to read the writing on the hangers or focus on the textures of the clothes. Alter your perspective until you've imagined your mental image from every angle.

Follow this same process with the other six ideas on the list, reflecting on how well you're able to visualise the objects, places, people and scenes you choose to represent each one. Do you find it easier to picture small objects or large ones, things or places, images from the front or above? Throughout this book you'll need to monitor your progress so that you know the natural strengths you can utilise as well as the areas you need to improve.

And when you've done it, see which images come back to your mind first. Can you remember all eight pictures, and the jobs they represented? You might be surprised at just how well you do, bearing in mind that all you did was spend some time thinking in pictures. Doing *anything* to information is always a valuable start, and creating visual imagery provides your mind with its most reliable building block. You're likely to find that you recall the pictures in roughly the original order, too. And when you do remember them, you know for certain that they're right – which is particularly useful when it comes to this sort of list. For example, did you have to go to the DIY store? What about the library? Should you pay the newsagent's bill or the vet's? The answers should come quickly and definitively, even after such a simple activity.

And of course images are the perfect starting-point because they can easily be linked together and fixed memorably in the brain.

Try it now: not a particularly complex or creative story, just a simple chain of connections based on details visible in each image.

Perhaps the bank teller is actually holding your dry cleaning. The tag on the bag is addressed to your child's teacher and fastened to a bunch of flowers, which seems to be dripping petrol on to a birthday card tucked inside a library book about vets ...

Now you should be able to remember all eight images even faster, backwards as well as forwards. If it was important to do the tasks in order, you'd know what to do after visiting the library or where you should have been before calling the school. Although it's easy to feel overwhelmed by all the things on your plate every day, and unable to use your memory to cope, you've just proved that efficient recall isn't far away. Remember: it starts with a decision to do it, a sensible plan, and then some vivid pictures that take seconds to paint. Once the images have been established they can be linked, grouped, removed, updated ... Priority tasks could be imagined in particularly bright colours, or you might add a vivid detail to each picture to tick it off when it was done. Try it now: imagine a bright red tick painted across the side of the bank, or see yourself imprinting the dry cleaning bag with a stamp saying *done*. Thinking in pictures immediately activates so many practical uses of your memory.

Sound

Stop for a moment. Listen. See how many sounds are entering your consciousness right now. Even if you're sitting alone in a quiet room, you might be surprised at just how many different noises are detectible. Close your eyes. Which sounds are nearest to you and which ones furthest away? What's the highest-pitched noise and what's the lowest? Are any of the sounds similar?

Now that you've tuned into the sense of hearing, try imagining some familiar sounds. If your mobile phone went off at this moment, what would you hear? Don't just think of the sound, really try to *hear* it. What about the sound of a baby crying, an ambulance racing by, or your mother talking to you? See how well you can imagine those distinct, familiar sounds. It's also worthwhile reflecting on how they would make you feel, because sounds have a particular power to alter our mood and provoke an instinctive reaction.

Here's a quick exercise to show you how sound can enrich memory. Below are six names. Say them to yourself a few times and listen carefully to the way they sound normally: each name as a whole, but also the individual syllables.

Ian Fish

Deborah Brown

Pareen Singh

Derek Marr

Tony O'Reilly

Wendy Cooper

Next, see if there are ways in which you could exaggerate the pronunciations to produce even more memorable sound effects. Spend a few moments playing around with the sounds, out loud and in your imagination.

You could imagine 'Ian' spoken in a high-pitched voice, the first syllable a squeaky door. With 'Fish', why not exaggerate the *sh* so that it sounds like a librarian telling noisy customers to 'shhhhhhhhhhh!'

Perhaps you repeat the last bit of 'Deborah': *Deborah-rah-rah-rah* ... You could make 'Singh' ring like a bell. Maybe you pronounce the first syllable of 'Tony' on a low note and the second one up high ...

And when you've made the noises out loud, read through the list again and hear all the sound effects purely in your 'mind's ear'.

Doing this when you met someone new would immediately boost your chances of remembering their name. You could imagine them making that noise when they told you their name, or the sound following them round like a character theme-tune in a video-game.

What happens if you blend sounds together? Could it create memorable connections, helping you to remember the names in order?

Try it out. Read through the list in your mind, repeating your sound effects and focusing on the end of one name and the start of the next.

And spend a moment returning to the to-do list you learnt earlier. Can you add an imagined sound to each of the eight images? Bring to mind the chink of the gold bars in the bank vault. Imagine talking to the teacher over the background noise of children playing. Hear the drip, drip, drip of the petrol. When your memory works well, a variety of senses are combined, so it can only help to add sense details whenever you can, providing you with more ways of connecting with stored information and bringing it back to life.

Taste

Memories of tastes are significant for survival. You need to remember how something *should* taste to know when it's gone bad and could harm you. Taste memories motivate you to hunt (or go to the supermarket) for things you've enjoyed and which have been good for you in the past. Your enjoyment of a plate of food begins before the first mouthful as you anticipate the tastes and feelings by accessing memories of previous meals.

Spend a moment thinking about your favourite food. How does it feel when you bite into it? What's its texture like in your mouth? Is it one flavour, or several combined? What emotions come to mind as you imagine devouring your own personal delicacy?

And what about your least-favourite taste? Maybe it's something you've always hated, something that once made you poorly, or even a food you've never actually tasted but the smell and appearance and just the thought of it turn your stomach. Notice how powerfully an imagined taste can affect your facial expression, the feeling in your mouth and your overall mood.

Practise imagining tastes and adding them to your memories with the following exercise. It's based on a trip around the town centre at Christmas. You've got seven presents to buy, and you can use tastes to help you remember them all.

dark chocolate   blue cheese   soap   toffee   book   chutney
gold chain

Take each item on the list and imagine biting into it. With some, that's straightforward; for others, it's bizarre. But for all of them it should certainly be memorable!

Imagine the snap of the bitter dark chocolate and the rich cocoa flavour filling your mouth as you chew. The blue cheese is crumbly and slightly sweet. The soap is ... disgusting, perfumed, cloying; but luckily it's replaced by rich, buttery toffee ...

When you've enjoyed (or endured) this entire taste experience, see how many of the seven Christmas presents you remember. Then read the list again, and this time focus on the contrasts between the flavours. The hard, bitter chocolate compared with the crumbly savoury/sweet cheese, then the chemical tang of the bubbly soap, followed by buttery toffee, dry and indigestible paper, into sharp, tangy chutney, and finally teeth-shattering, metallic gold.

Now how many of the seven can you remember, and how close can you come to the original order?

And could you add tastes to the to-do list? A baby would try to explore the money and the dry cleaning and everything else with its mouth, so why don't you try including the sense of taste as another layer in your memory making?

Touch

The next sense is quite a challenge: touch. In reality, it's usually very easy to tell the difference between the feel of a silk gown and a bristly nailbrush – but in your imagination? It's difficult to re-create sensations in detail, although it can be done, and it can really help you to remember.

Touch affects emotions powerfully. An icy bathroom floor, a calming hug, the kick from an electric fence. The impact is immediate, and using touch and texture in your memory techniques can help to create the all-important connection required to make information truly memorable.

Have a look around the room you're in now. Imagine touching some of the things you can see: a range of different objects, fabrics, natural substances and manufactured materials. Do they feel rough or smooth, warm or cold, dry, sticky, hard, dusty, sharp? You'll find that your fingertips feel alive even though you're doing the touching in your mind. Then try touching some of the same things for real. How accurate was your imagination?

Here are six DIY tasks to sort out before your house goes on the market next week. Use them to practise remembering through texture and touch.

- Finish grouting the tiles.
- Repair the brickwork.
- Glue the drawer.
- Oil the door hinge.
- Tack the carpet.
- Paint the skirting board.

Start by imagining the smooth, cold texture of the new grouting. Then bring to mind the rough surface of the brick wall, the feel of sticky glue on your fingers ... Create a 'touch memory' for each job, and then see what happens when you connect the textures together: squeezing grouting between the bricks, which are covered in glue mixed with oil, with tacks floating in it that have been gloss painted.

Return to the to-do list earlier in the chapter and see whether you can add touch into the mix of sense triggers: the texture of crisp banknotes, the thick, sticky feel of petrol, the sharp edge of the greetings card ...

Smell

Smells evoke memories with a particular intensity. Like touch, they can be hard to imagine, although their impact on emotion can help. Spend a moment bringing to mind a few favourite smells and some that you hate; then some smells that take you back to happy times; and any others that connect you with unpleasant memories. Your feelings will help to re-create the smells in your mind, the reverse of what happens so often in real life.

Other smells are instantly recognisable but hard to pinpoint. It's great memory training to try to pick out individual smells in a kitchen, garden or even a busy office.

See how quickly you can name them, and be alert to any memories they evoke.

Imagine you had to buy the following ingredients for your Christmas cake recipe:

- raisins
- lemon
- brandy
- nutmeg
- mixed spices

To practise incorporating the powerful sense of smell into your learning, try to imagine the smell of each of these items in turn. Use your other senses to help: imagine seeing the food, touching it, tasting it ... and then allow the *smell* of it to fill your mind, along with any feelings or emotions it activates.

You'll probably find it hard to escape memories of Christmas, since many of these smells are particularly associated with that time of year, and the cake as a whole should take you back to moments from Christmas past.

And to stretch your ability to connect information together, to balance your sensitive, experimental, right-brained thinking with left-brained logic and order, have a go at blending these scents – just like a perfume manufacturer blends individual ingredients to make the perfect fragrance. In this case, it might make for a rather unusual aftershave ... but a very evocative smell of Christmas. Imagine this was a very carefully designed scent, beginning with sugary raisins, going into sharp, citrus lemon, blending with some heady fumes of brandy, being softened by sweet nutmeg and then finished with exotic mixed spice. Can you tell a 'smell story' and explore yet another way of using your whole brain brilliantly?

Finally, go back to the to-do list that's already been enriched with four types of sense information. See if smells can make your imagery and ideas even more memorable: sniff the money, check the dry cleaning smells fresh ... go through the list one last time, making use of all the other memory triggers you've attached as you add a final layer of connection and significance.

Total recall

As you spend a moment thinking about the list of jobs you need to remember, you may well find examples of humour, horror, surrealism; things to attract and things to repel; excitement, violence, action, surprise ... With strong images as the foundation, covered in layers of sense triggers, the original information has been brought to life memorably in your imagination – but you've also given it logic, 'imagining' it into a very robust order. The pictures tell a story, but the sounds, textures, tastes and smells also provide clues about how the ideas fit together.

In this chapter you've seen how right- and left-brain thinking can come together to make memories, consciously, creatively and consistently. Your imagination lets you use all your senses to enrich the dullest information; those senses themselves can help to knit together the individual details; and your logical left brain joins the party by creating stories and patterns and making connections that will keep the memories firmly fixed. Suddenly your memory is tapping into your strongest emotions to allow learning to hit a new level.

In the next chapter you'll see more of what you can achieve with this sort of whole-brain approach. All the techniques you've practised in this chapter will be invaluable as you learn about the most important ancient memory system of all: the one that will revolutionise the way you think and learn.

 **brilliant** recap

- Your right brain specialises in imagination, your left brain in logic.

- Brilliant memory involves using both sides together.

- Mix the liberated learning of children with the ordered approach of adults.

- Strengthen your senses and incorporate them all in your learning.

- Emotional reactions activate lasting memories.

PART 2

Applications

CHAPTER 6

Learning lists

Memory is the treasure house of
the mind.

Thomas Fuller

In this chapter you will learn:

- that the Greeks and Romans invented a way to remember anything
- why the system of *loci* matches the way your memory works
- how to turn familiar places into mental buildings and routes
- strategies for remembering shopping lists, instructions, directions, talks ...
- where else this technique might take you, with a bit of imagination

For centuries we've known that place triggers memory. Going back somewhere – for real, or in the mind – can remind you of detailed information from decades before, peeling back multiple layers from the past and activating your memory in rich and vibrant ways.

 In Ancient Rome, Quintilian wrote about the powerful connection between memory and place: '*for when we return to a place after a considerable absence, we not merely recognise the place itself, but remember things that we did there, and recall the persons whom we met and even the unuttered thoughts that passed through our minds when we were there before*'.

The Greeks and Romans put this intriguing aspect of memory to use. They developed a system that made it possible to learn large amounts of information with remarkable ease. It helped them to explore, remember and communicate their ideas in truly impressive ways – and the good news is that it still works brilliantly today. It makes your memory work efficiently, flexibly and creatively. It even comes complete with a user-guide.

The Journey System could be exactly what your memory's been waiting for.

The Journey System

Ancient origins

The Greeks had the idea first but it was the Romans who developed it into a practical memory tool. It's a simple concept with infinite applications: you use the places you know to hold the information you want to know. Familiar buildings and journeys become mental structures which can be filled with memorable information, rediscovered when you return there in your mind. Cicero, one of its most skilful users, explained the system in a nutshell: *The order of the places will preserve the order of the things to be remembered.*

 **definition**

Loci

Loci is the plural of *locus*, the Latin word for 'place'. This powerful memory technique is often called 'the system of loci', based on mental tours around carefully built and delicately decorated places.

Rooms and routes

It's also known as the *Roman Room System*, reflecting another take on one key idea. You can use a single room, several rooms within a building, landmarks on a journey – even tours of entire cities – to give your memory the sort of frameworks it finds so useful for storing information. Everything you want to know is converted into images, using all the tried-and-tested strategies for making them memorable, and then those images are arranged around the rooms or routes you've set out in your mind.

Global learning in action

Memory journeys work particularly well because they get both halves of your brain – both sides of your thinking – working together.

There's clear, left-brained logic in the arrangement of places, allowing you to move forwards or backwards through the information, to pick out particular details and to add or delete images whenever you want. But there's also a wonderful amount of right-brained imagination involved in creating memorable pictures and fixing them into place with colour, action, comedy and chaos. The imagery promotes creative connections; so, as well as remembering the original material, you're also exploring it on an exciting new level.

Although you'll be using the journey system to boost your memory in the modern world, you've been left some useful advice from the distant past. The anonymous Roman text *Ad Herrenium* outlined some practical rules:

- Your *loci* – the different areas of rooms and buildings or the landmarks on journeys – need to be deserted or solitary. They start empty, ready to be filled with images, but they should stay uncluttered and clear in your mind's eye.

- To avoid confusion, each stopping-place also needs to be different from the rest. Ancient users of this technique were very creative with furniture and décor to make every *locus* unique.

- You need to have 'checkpoints' along the way to make sure you don't skip images, and to help you access individual images. The Roman tradition was to 'tag' every fifth and tenth *locus* in some memorable way.

- It's a good idea to have fairly regular intervals between *loci*. Your memory journeys should be fluent and steady, with no cramped movements or giant leaps from one image to the next.

- Be careful with the size of *loci* – not too big or too small – and make sure they're well lit, allowing you to see the images you've stored there in all their glory.

You need to see how good this system is for yourself. To get you started, here's a ready-made route for you to use: a ten-point journey around a grand country house. After all, if you're going to design some mental architecture from scratch, you might as well make it beautiful, spacious and calm.

Spend some time getting to know the place. Take a walk around it in your imagination.

Locus 1: Driveway
Your journey starts on the wide driveway leading up to the house. Imagine the pristine white gravel beneath your feet.

Locus 2: Front door
Stand on the stone step in front of huge oak-panelled doors, preparing to step inside.

Locus 3: Entrance hall
You're in the house now, standing in the middle of a large, galleried entrance hall, gazing at the beautiful works of art on the walls. An open door on the right takes you to ...

Locus 4: Cloakroom
This is where you hang your coat on a fancy hook and put your

bag on one of the polished wooden shelves, before walking through to …

Locus 5: Sitting room

The furniture here is suitably sumptuous, so take a moment to relax on a long, velvet sofa. And since this is the fifth stopping-place on the route, stay a little longer than normal – and notice the number 5 that's been carved into each of the sofa's wooden legs.

Locus 6: Dining room

From the sitting room, a door takes you into the long, formal dining room. The mahogany table here is laid for a banquet – but you're more interested in what goes on behind the scenes, so step into …

Locus 7: Kitchen

A big house needs a big kitchen. This one is equipped with every possible appliance, everything brand new and immaculately clean.

Locus 8: Staircase

From the kitchen, a set of double doors takes you to a wide, sweeping staircase and up towards the first floor of the house. Feel the quality of the carpet under your feet as you climb the stairs and reach …

Locus 9: Bathroom

This is the first room you come to at the top of the stairs, and it's the most luxurious bathroom you've ever seen, with solid marble surfaces and gleaming gold fittings.

Locus 10: Bedroom

The final stopping-point on your tour of the house is a bedroom, complete with stately four-poster bed, antique furniture – and a large number 10 embroidered on the quilt.

Now go back through the ten *loci* from memory. There's a very clear path to follow, taking you from the first place, the driveway, all the way to the last, the bedroom. As you imagine standing in each location, bring to mind all the details you can. Check that each *locus* is different, with space to be filled, uncluttered and well lit; that you know where to find the mid-point, *locus* 5; and that the tour is a well-spaced, regular route from start to finish.

---

brilliant tip

To check you're confident with a new memory building or journey, always take the tour *backwards*, from *locus 10* to *locus 1* – and when you can do that, you're ready to put it to use.

Seven steps to success

Remember the seven key stages of the memory process? Your memory journey is the perfect opportunity to put them all into practice:

Start by *deciding* to memorise the ten items on a shopping list:

carrots   strawberries   pineapple-juice   cake   bread
porridge   sugar   jam   bacon   butter

Your *strategy* is simple: to invent a powerful image for each product and then position them all around the country house, one in each room.

As you *visualise* the images and then organise them around the route, make everything as *personal* and *exaggerated* as possible.

Imagine ...

... standing on the driveway and seeing hundreds of bright orange carrots sprouting up through the white gravel. You bite the top off

one of the crunchy carrots before crunching along the gravel to the front door – which is shaped like a strawberry. It's the same colour, too, because someone has smeared it with sticky strawberry juice, which gets all over your hands as you open the door and walk into the entrance hall. This room is swimming with pineapple juice, almost reaching the paintings on the wall. You're not a good swimmer and it's scary as you paddle and splash your way through the thick yellow juice to the other side of the room. In the cloakroom, an expensive cake has been squashed on to each hook, and you have to move a cake to put your bag down on the shelf. Brushing cake crumbs off your hands, you walk into the sitting room – and feel very relieved that this part of the house is warm and cosy and smells of freshly baked bread: probably because all of the furniture here is made *from large loaves of bread. Pause for a moment, wondering who's carved the number 5 into the breadstick sofa legs … before walking into the dining room. You're horrified to see that there seems to have been a food fight. Porridge is dripping from the table, the ceiling, even the chandeliers. Do you dare to taste a bit of the cold, lumpy porridge? The dining room leads to the kitchen, which is bright and white – mainly because every surface here is covered in a dusting of sugar. You draw your name in the sugary worktop (and lick it to take away the taste of the porridge!) before heading for the stairs. Someone's piled jars of jam on the stairs and you almost get to the top without knocking them over … but then you catch one with your foot, that jar hits another jar, and suddenly they're all tumbling down the staircase like dominoes, smashing and covering you and the expensive carpet with thick, sticky blackcurrant jam. The bathroom would be a good place to clean up, but the sink is blocked with a huge pile of bacon. There's bacon filling the bath, too, and although you do your best to clear the cold, greasy mass of meat, it's stuck fast. Exhausted, you're really glad to see the tall four-poster in the middle of the bedroom next door. You leap on to it – but instead of sinking into the soft mattress and comfy covers you slide straight off. Someone has smeared butter across the quilt, giving the embroidered number 10 a glistening sheen but making it absolutely impossible for you to get into bed for a well-deserved rest, however hard you try …*

You've now *organised* the information carefully in your memory. And the seventh step is to *practise*: so now close your eyes and go back through the ten rooms of this stately home, letting all the clues you've left remind you of the ten items of shopping you need to buy.

You can often speed up your recall by asking questions. It's what you do naturally when you visit new places, and in this case there's no shortage of things to be curious about! What's here, why is it that colour, where's it coming from, who did that, what's going to happen next ...?

When you're ready, see what it feels like to be completely in control of your memory. Get your country house to 'tell' you the ten items in perfect order – forwards, and then backwards. What was the fifth thing on the list? What came before the pineapple-juice? Was coffee on the list? What about sugar, lemons, jam?

Just the beginning

You've put in the effort to erect a whole building in your imagination, so why not use it again and learn some new information straight away?

In ancient times, the *loci* were often compared to wax tablets, easily wiped clean of information and reused, and you'll find that this happens remarkably easily – if you want it to. But in this case, keep the original images – the shopping list – in place, and use them to give your memory even more to hold on to. Each new image can be connected to whatever you've just put in, building up multi-layered memories that have an even better chance of staying put.

Here's a second list to learn: ten items of clothing. Perhaps you need to buy them, or talk about them, or remember them for a fashion show or school play.

socks   skirt   coat   gloves   trousers   ball-gown   scarf   shirt hat   shoes

Just follow the lead of the ancients, remember all your seven steps to success, and have a go yourself at creating vivid mental images to activate your memory. Enjoy exercising both sides of your brain.

Perhaps you pull a sock on to each carrot, wipe off the strawberry-juice with a new, clean skirt, wear the padded coat to help you float in the pool of pineapple ... It shouldn't be hard to create surreal images, with you at the centre of every strange scene.

When you've fixed all ten new images in place, practise remembering them on their own – the gloves, the trousers, the ball-gown – but also see what happens when you juggle them with the food you remembered first. What clothing was in the same room as the bacon? What came before the room that smelt of bread? You might have got used to thinking of your memory as disorganised and lazy, but look what happens when you start using it well! You can learn and remember with phenomenal precision – in fact, the more information you absorb, the easier it becomes to keep everything in place, each image connecting to others in ways that you can really use.

Could you even add a third layer of memories to this creative collection? There's certainly room in your mind: just be confident that the amount of information you're learning doesn't matter as much as the way in which you learn it. You know the order of rooms; you now have even more 'hooks' on which the new images can hang; and you've got your brain firing on all cylinders, ready to keep learning powerfully and precisely ... so give it a go!

Here are the ten animals you want to write about in your science essay, or discuss in your talk on conservation, or visit as you walk around the zoo with your kids ...

zebra   lion   meerkat   eagle   giraffe   beetle   monkey snake   mouse   rhino

So now can you remember three lists, thirty items, forwards, backwards, from any particular starting-point ... finding food and clothing by naming an animal ... seeing three images in the seventh room ... saying the food that went with the trousers and the clothing that came before the room full of porridge ...?

Has your memory ever felt this brilliant before?

Home sweet home

If you're going to design your own set of *loci*, where better to start than at home?

Follow the four steps below to create a memory framework based on the building you know best: the place where you live. It doesn't matter if it's a house or an apartment, a cottage or a castle; you can turn any kind of home into a solid structure to store images of anything. You make the most of all your associations with the real location, and get a real boost to your confidence from transporting yourself to a place that's familiar and safe.

Step 1: Overview
Before you choose the ten memory 'zones' inside, spend a moment thinking about the *sort* of places they're going to be and

how they'll be organised. Trust the wisdom of the Romans and try to spread them throughout your home, making good use of all the space available. You can choose rooms, passageways, staircases, yards, gardens, lofts, roof-tops – even individual pieces of furniture. It all depends on the options offered by the real location, and how you can make the most of them.

Step 2: Route planning

When you've considered the 'big picture', start to focus on the details. Choose ten very clear, very different spaces within your home and sort them into a route that makes sense. Write it out on paper – as a numbered list or map. You need to be absolutely sure about the order of stopping-points on your mental journey, from the first *locus* to the last. Keep it as realistic as you can, making the most of your instinctive knowledge of the real place – but also breaking the rules here and there if you find a wall in your way or need to go up a floor without any stairs …

brilliant tip

It can help to imagine you're filming a mental movie. Your camera can go through walls, squeeze into the smallest bits of furniture or even swing outside the house to look in: whatever makes it easier to travel fluently from the start of the tour to the finish.

Here are two example routes – although of course yours will be completely unique.

1 Front garden
2 Hallway
3 Living room
4 Dining room
5 Kitchen

6   Staircase

7   Landing

8   Children's room

9   Master bedroom

10 En-suite bathroom

1   Lift

2   Apartment door

3   Coat rack

4   Sitting area

5   Dining table

6   Food cupboard

7   Fridge

8   Shower room

9   Bedroom

10 Balcony

Step 3: Room design

Now visit each room, area or piece of furniture in turn in your mind's eye (or movie camera's lens) and visualise these spaces in as much detail as you can. Set up the viewing angle for each one – and stick to it, so that each *locus* looks basically the same every time. Remember the Roman tips about good lighting and staying free from clutter, but make a note of any useful features you find. Distinctive details can become very useful 'hooks' for the images you create. Make sure there's something in the fifth area to remind you it's the halfway point on the tour.

Step 4: Rehearsal

Finally, make the whole journey in your mind. Visualise yourself standing in each of the ten *loci* in turn, looking from the same angle every time and focusing on as many details as you can.

View your mental movie to make sure the route from start to finish is crystal clear – and check that you can also rewind it and move backwards through the memory zones.

⤢ brilliant exercise

Put your 'home journey' into action straight away. Here are ten bits of information you might want to remember about your family's busy life this week. Turn them all into images, then fix each image into its 'slot' in the route.

1   Send out party invitations.
2   Book dentist's appointments.
3   Pay the electricity bill.
4   Check on your next-door neighbour.
5   Order new curtains.
6   Discuss summer holiday plans.
7   Mend the shower.
8   Pick up dry cleaning.
9   Wash the car.
10   Invite the children's friends for tea.

Make use of everything you've learnt so far about memory as you take ownership of this information. Give everything significance, make it connect powerfully with you, and follow those all-important seven steps to set up artificial memories that the ancient masters would be proud of!

You might imagine standing in a garden littered with old birthday invitations, or seeing that the front door has been decorated with party balloons and banners. Perhaps the hallway has become the dentist's waiting room, or maybe the door to your apartment is now shaped like an open mouth. Pick one aspect of each note on the list – electricity, your neighbour's face, some floral curtains – and exaggerate it, give it impact in any way you can, and fix it into the next place on the tour. You can add more details if you need to – a brochure about your chosen holiday spot; the particular part needed to mend the shower – but make sure the 'big idea' of each reminder is clear: the bags of dry cleaning in the children's toy-box, the dirty car being washed on your bed, the kids' tea-party going on in your en-suite …

When you've created ten images and fixed them in place, spend a moment going back through the *loci* and strengthening the memories. Which senses and emotions would enrich the journey? How could you make better use of the distinctive details already there? Could any of the images be confusing, or are they all as clear and powerful as possible?

And then, see if it's worked. Move fluently through the ten spaces in your mental framework, rediscovering the image clues you've left for yourself and saying exactly what they mean.

---

brilliant dos and don'ts

Do

✔ *Do … give a running commentary on the journey.* Talking to yourself can make sure you go the right way and trigger memories of key images, especially when you ask the right questions. 'I'm through the apartment door and I go straight to … the coat rack. Why are all my electrical gadgets hanging there?' 'So let's go upstairs … and I know I have to be careful here, because … yes, there are buckets and spades all up the staircase …'

✔ *Do … improve the images every time you remember them.* This is the self-supporting brilliance of memory at its best. Imagine your reactions to finding these strange things around your home. Picture yourself doing something at each point in the journey, strengthening your memories of whatever's there.

Don't

✗ *Don't … go too fast.* There's a temptation to rush around the route, gathering up all the imagery you placed inside – and

missing out key *loci* in the process. Keep visualising yourself
making the journey for real and you won't forget to look in
that cupboard or to stop on those stairs.

✗ *Don't … worry if you come to a gap.* It's unlikely, the system
is so strong; but if you do find you can't remember what's in
a particular place, leave it for now and continue with your
journey. The rest of the information should still be in place,
all held in the right slots. Something later may well remind
you of what's in the 'empty' room, especially when you take
the tour in reverse. Keep asking questions and following any
associations – even vague ones like 'there was something
funny here …' or 'why can I smell burning?' Don't give up until
all the clues you created lead you to the memory store.

brilliant impact

As well as lists of words, objects and jobs, you can use memory journeys to
remember instructions and directions. When the order of your information is
so important, the route system is ideal. Even abstract ideas like 'turn right'
or 'fold lengthwise' can be turned into something concrete and memorable
and fixed in place in your creative mind. The structured mental journey
keeps you on track as you follow the instructions in precise order, forwards
or backwards, and you can add as much detail as you need to complete the
task brilliantly.

What about adding another set of information to the journey
you just used? Try coming up with images for the following
travel directions, then put them into the first five *loci* around
your home. Combine them with the to-do list pictures already
there to create some surreal and unforgettable scenes.

1   Turn right.

2   Go to the top of the hill.

3   Turn left.

4   Go past the cemetery.

5   At the school, take the second road on the right.

To remember which way to turn, you could fix image-clues in place on the right or left side of your memory space. So a huge model hand on the right of the garden would remind you to turn right. Maybe there's a magnet on the far-left coat hook, pulling you in that direction. If you found your kitchen had been transformed into a school, and noticed not one but two flashing signs pointing out of the window on the right, you'd think: 'definitely second right at the school'.

And have a go with some practical instructions: the start of a cake recipe. Carry on from zone 6 in your home route and add images telling you to …

6   Heat the oven to Gas Mark 4.

7   Butter a cake tin.

8   Beat together the butter and sugar.

9   Add a few drops of vanilla.

10   Mix in the flour.

Use your artificial memory the first few times you make the journey or bake the cake and soon the physical actions will come naturally – but you'll always have some detailed reminders ready if you ever get stuck.

Working memory

To round off this chapter, build yourself one more memory route – based on the place where you work. Once again it's just common sense to start using your most familiar structures to manage your mind. They're ready-made memory stores, full of powerful associations and connections. Follow the steps above, take your time to get the details right, and set yourself up with another ten-*locus* framework ready to absorb all the images you create – and to keep you in complete control of your memory.

In the following chapters you'll find out how to turn the most specific information – detailed facts and figures for every purpose – into vivid imagery to slot into this and many other kinds of memory frame. But for now, how about practising with the list below, which could be:

- subject-areas for a team-building talk
- topics for a night-class essay
- revision for a sports quiz
- reminders about the exercise plan that you're definitely going to stick to this time ...

It's actually the ten events in the Olympic decathlon, in the order they happen: useful general knowledge, but it's also there to get you thinking about the sort of real information that you could start remembering right now, using the power of memory journeys to make an impact in so many different areas of your life.

Decathlon disciplines

1   100 metres
2   Long jump
3   Shot put
4   High jump
5   400 metres
6   Hurdles
7   Discus

8 Pole vault

9 Javelin

10 1500 metres

Use this exercise to practise everything you've learnt about memory so far. Turn the information in front of you into memorable images and fix them all firmly into your new memory store. Make the experience active and personal and unforgettable.

Maybe you start by joining the sprinters in their race across the car-park, then break the long-jump record as you leap across the lobby, before heaving a huge metal ball on to the receptionist's desk …

What next?

So, how can you start putting memory journeys to use in your real life? What are the best ways to learn all the detailed information you need, at work, in your studies, during your social life – and to stay on top of all the challenges you face from day to day? What would happen if each image you created was just the starting-point for a memory story, so that every room in your ordered imagination was filled with as much information as you chose to store? What would *that* mean for your general knowledge, communication skills, learning power – and overall confidence to succeed?

Memory is boosted by questions of every kind. The good news about *these* questions is that the answers really are life changing – and they're coming next.

brilliant recap

- Since ancient times, physical locations have been used to manage memories.
- Memory journeys bring together both sides of the brain.
- Use familiar routes to trigger memories of new information.
- Fill rooms with memory clues that activate senses and feelings.
- Make sure your mental journeys match all the principles of brilliant memory.

CHAPTER 7

Words and ideas

The palest ink is better than the best memory.

Chinese proverb

In this chapter you will learn:

- a new way of handling all the words you want to know
- how to create lasting memories of abstract ideas
- the 'active reading' technique for remembering complex texts
- strategies to improve your spelling and widen your vocabulary
- techniques for memorising foreign words and phrases

Sometimes it feels like you're drowning in a sea of words. So much of the material you need to remember comes as text: revision notes, journal pages, web encyclopaedias, vocabulary lists. In daily life you're expected to retain tiny details of spellings and subtle differences in definitions and meanings, but also to manage the vast stores of information contained in long and complex passages. Words often present you with abstract ideas that give your brain very little to go on. And as well as feeling more confident in your own language, how much more might you achieve if only you could learn foreign words in a way that really worked?

Modern technology delivers us more words than ever before: verbal information that we need to know, plus a wealth of material that we'd *love* to learn and put to use. But what's easy to read on paper or screen can quickly fade when you try to inscribe it in your mind. To succeed in so many areas of life, you need a range of techniques for remembering words efficiently and effectively – and then using them brilliantly.

Continue what you've started

You should already have realised the possibilities. In your training so far, most of the material you've practised with has been in the form of words: random words in pairs, groups and lists, and more meaningful ideas expressed in single words, phrases or sentences. You've got used to developing the strongest images for real things, and you've learnt how to think creatively about more abstract information and to turn that, too, into powerful pictures. But now it's time to start working with the words of real life – which involves looking at language in a new way and starting to do some very powerful things with it in your mind.

brilliant tip

Imagine you're a crossword compiler, analysing and dissecting every word to turn it into something clever and memorable. In the world of crosswords, a river can be a flower, because it *flows*. A capital letter is a London landlord. If a plane crashes anywhere it's likely to be Nepal (anag.). And when Brian is poorly inside at the junction, it's *brilliant* (brILLianT). Crossword experts are used to playing around with how words look and sound, finding puns, creating anagrams, spotting words-within-words, and using every kind of abbreviation, shorthand and clever clue to explore language in exciting ways. And that's a great way to remember words, too, because it's active, creative, organised and engaging. It brings words to life.

Dismantle the following seven words and see what images you can find inside. They're seven fairly abstract ideas, but *very* important ones: the seven key stages of the memory process. You've been reading these words and using these concepts for a while, but now it's time to build them into your brain.

deciding   strategising   visualising   personalising
exaggerating   organising   practising

To begin with, spend a moment thinking about the real meaning of each word. What does this idea 'look like'? If you were illustrating it in a children's book or giving it an image in a business presentation, what sort of picture would you use?

Then start to look for new ideas. Focus on what the word really looks like, how it sounds and what it reminds you of. See what happens when you change a letter here or there, swap vowel sounds, split up the syllables. Remember: you're looking for anything that might suggest some memorable new imagery, lifting your thinking to the level where it works best – but eventually leading your brain back to this word on the page.

Make sure you have a go yourself before reading the suggestions below. Don't worry if you find it hard. It's a new way of thinking about words, but you'll quickly get better with practice and start spotting connections and clues in seconds. You don't need to turn the whole word into something new: just look for something inside it that will trigger your memory.

Deciding

The real meaning could be illustrated by a ballot paper, a judge giving his verdict or a Roman emperor's down-turned thumb. And being more creative with the word, you might think about *cider*, use an association with *Deeside* in Scotland, or make something out of the first three letters: Dec for *December*. Make the most of whatever ideas come to mind. It's great to have a range of options when you come to organising your images and fixing them in your mind.

Strategising

Perhaps you think about military leaders making their battle plans, or friends playing a strategy board game; and then play around with the sound of the word to make 'straight edges' – or spot the *rat* hiding in there.

Visualising

This could be a sportsman seeing himself 'in the zone' or a fortune-teller imagining the future; or, change the sound of the first syllable to give you a racing-driver's *visor*, or the spelling, to make it *fizz* …

Personalising

You could think about a personalised number-plate, a completely customised car – or someone *pursing* their lips, a *purse* or a *purring* cat.

Exaggerating

The real word might suggest a caricature painter or a mime artist. With a bit of creative thinking you could also use images of *eggs*, something *hexagonal*, or someone *gyrating*.

Organising

A tidy desk or perfectly organised Zen garden; and maybe an *organist* wearing *organza*.

Practising

Your first thoughts might be of sports stars training or actors in the middle of a dress rehearsal, and then your creative brain might suggest *packed ice* or *pricked icing*.

Looking at words like this gives you a wide selection of images: some based on real meanings, but others produced by your creative brain to enrich the memories you make. So, when it's time to arrange them around one of your memory routes, you have some truly striking scenes:

... a judge drunk on cider

... a strategy game being played by rats

... a fortune-teller wearing a visor

... a personalised number-plate fastened to a purse

... a mime artist gyrating

... a tidy desk being played like an organ

... a team training-session held on packed ice

Of course these are just suggestions. The details visualised by every person who tries this task will be different – and they *need* to be: personalised by you, exaggerated as much as you possibly can, and made to match *your* unique brain.

You might imagine:

- the cider-loving judge in your front garden
- the rats sorting their strategy in the hallway of your house
- the visor-wearing fortune-teller relaxing in the living room
- a personalised purse on every chair in the dining-room ...

And you'd remember it all because you'd have:

- actively engaged with the information you wanted to learn
- set up general reminders of the big themes
- left yourself specific clues about the exact words you're learning
- given your memory various ways to reconnect with the original ideas

Push yourself to remember these words in a way that really works. As well as proving that even abstract ideas can be given powerful, precise image clues, it teaches you the seven-step memory method that underpins all the training in this book.

🔎 brilliant impact

When you get into the habit of looking at language in this detailed and creative way, you'll find your overall confidence with words improves. As well as strengthening your spelling, expanding your vocabulary and pushing you to try out new languages, this approach sets up your brain to solve puzzles, make jokes, read between the lines – and to choose and use your own words better than ever before.

How far you've come from simply reading something through a few times and hoping it might stick! This new approach to learning puts you in complete control, leaving you with multi-layered memories – the multiple connections that your brain relishes – and a clear path through all the rich and vivid reminders that you've arranged carefully around your brain. It's like a 3D film, using two cameras at once to create richness and depth. In your mental movie studio, real meanings and creative interpretations – the logical left and the imaginative right – are the two angles that come together to bring your learning to life.

Memory texts

When you know how to turn individual words – any words at all – into memorable images, you're ready to start learning whole documents: essay notes, revision texts, finance magazines, history books … whatever you need to know, in as much detail as you want to remember it.

And that's something very important to consider when you're *deciding* to use your memory and *strategising* your approach: how much of your document do you really need to know? Will it be enough to remember the key points? Do you need to learn particular names, facts or quotations? Is the order in which things appear important? Learning enough of a magazine article to discuss it at an ideas meeting at work will be very different from studying textbooks before your seminar or memorising the structure and detail of an exam essay. Careful thought at this early stage will pay dividends during the rest of the memory-making process.

brilliant tip

How often do you find yourself looking at a document but not really reading it? It's tempting to read something passively and then tick it off as a job done, even though you know none of it has gone in – but that's such a waste of time. Give up on aimless reading. Learn how to remember texts properly, be strategic and invest time in the active approach that will make all the difference.

Key points

Start by highlighting the most important bits in the text: the main ideas that will form the skeleton structure of your learning. If you were making prompt cards for a talk, or writing subheadings into an article, what would the key points be? Doing this ensures that you understand what you're reading, so you're already activating your memory – and you'll find that useful images already start to emerge. Use the '3D' technique you've been exploring to create both literal and creative illustrations, getting your whole brain involved and giving yourself a variety of connections back to the central ideas.

brilliant tip

If possible, highlight key words on the document itself or write in your own sub-headings, either in gaps between paragraphs or alongside sections of text. And while you're doing so, don't be afraid to use colour, draw cartoons, put in some of your own thoughts and start making the printed page eye-catching, unusual, personal and memorable. Later, as well as using your specific strategies to learn the text, you might be surprised at just how well you remember what you did to the words on the page.

Set up the structure …

Once you've got your key points, and each point has been given some powerful images, slot them into a memory journey, one point per place. In that way, even if you do nothing else, you'll know all the main ideas in the right order. Practise travelling through the *loci* in your mind's eye and fix this skeleton structure into your memory.

… then add the details

Now you can add as much extra detail as you want, creating new images to include in each *locus*. There's a key idea in each one, but soon there can be a whole collection of detailed ideas leading from it. This is where the storytelling technique comes back into play. Within the overall structure of a memory journey, each image can be the starting-point for a mini memory scene or story. In that way, you can quickly go to a particular place in your memory building, trigger your memory about a big theme – and have all the details about it at your fingertips.

Here's how it might look in action, using a textbook chapter about wines of the world. If you were studying this information for a night-class test, a social-club talk or to prepare for a real wine tasting, the names of particular wines might well be your main themes – to which you could add as much detail as you wished.

So, you'd start by reading the text carefully and highlighting the key ideas: the ones to turn into the 'headline' images for each *locus* in your mental journey. Perhaps you'd pick out six main wines and focus on the order in which you wanted to talk or write about them. Then you'd simply put image clues about them into the first six *loci* of a memory journey.

Beaujolais *Perhaps a wine bottle wearing a bow and looking very jolly.*

Zinfandel *A Zen fan called Del?*

Pinot Noir *Pinning a note to Noah.*

Sauvignon Blanc *Savage Sophie on Mont Blanc.*

Pinot Grigio *Pinocchio the Gigolo.*

Chardonnay *Cher and Donnie (Osmond?), charred onions, a shard of glass on some hay ...* or whatever associations your brain squeezes out of the word.

brilliant tip

If you already know something about the *real* meanings of words, make sure you use that to give you some specific images too. But this technique works even with material that's brand new to you. Get into the habit of pinning images on to words you've never even heard of before and you'll be a step ahead when it comes to learning foreign languages, names, jargon and all the other verbal material that doesn't come with meaning 'attached'.

As you slot these particular images into a memory journey – one based, for example, on your local supermarket – you might notice that the wine bottles stacked up in the car-park are all wearing bow-ties and making jolly noises: *Beaujolais*. By the automatic doors, maybe a group of Zen fans are all chanting the name of their leader, 'Del, Del, Del ...' *Zinfandel*. In the vegetable section, a shop assistant is pinning a note on Noah, who's sitting in his Ark on top of the carrots: *Pinot Noir* ...

With those main images in place you'd be ready to insert extra details. Reading your textbook carefully, you might choose the following facts to add:

- Beaujolais is the name of a wine-making region of France.
- It produces mostly red wine.
- Zinfandel wine is known for its rich, dark colour.
- This grape grows best in climates that are warm, but not hot.
- Pinot Noir is a difficult grape to grow.
- It's one of the more expensive varieties.
- This wine is known for its berry flavours.

... and, to do so, you'd simply return to each *locus* and add more images to trigger your memory.

Maybe you'd visualise the wine-bottles in the car-park surrounded by villages and fields, and the whole region stamped with the distinctive red, white and blue Tricolour flag of France. Then the red colour could seep out of the flag and turn *everything* red, including the bottles and their jolly bow-ties.

The Zen fans by the doors could all look particularly rich and be dressed in dark suits. You could zoom in your mental movie camera to see the beads of sweat on their faces. They like being warm, but not hot, and soon they're all taking off their dark jackets to keep the temperature just right.

In the vegetable aisle, perhaps Noah is finding it difficult to plant grapes on his Ark. You could picture a very expensive price-tag attached to each grape. Maybe they're *so* expensive that Noah replaces them with strawberries, blackberries, raspberries ...

Active reading

This is word learning at its best. By this stage, after beginning with the printed page, you'd have extracted the key points, created main images to put into a memory story, then pulled out just the right amount of detail to incorporate into each scene. And when you walked back through the journey in your mind you'd rediscover the key points, and each one would trigger its own mini memory-store of extra facts.

With practice you just get used to reading texts in this way – at least when you want to learn them. You can still read for pleasure, skim articles or learn just the top level of information. But when you need to – when you *decide* to – you can work with texts on a new level, adding layers of imagination and organisation that let you explore and remember them brilliantly.

⤴ **brilliant** impact

One big advantage of remembering like this is that the learning isn't fixed, as can often be the case with learning-by-repetition. Existing images can be tweaked, new ones can be added, and each *locus* has endless space as you do more research and want to remember more.

Put all these techniques to the test now by absorbing information from the text below. To help you become even more of an expert on wine, here's the first part of a guide to wine tasting – for you to read, actively, and transform into something truly memorable. You've been shown the steps, now simply put them into action.

Step 1: Read the text carefully, looking for the key points. (For example, *Chardonnay*.)

Step 2: Create images for the main ideas, reflecting anything you know about their real meanings. (Maybe a bottle of your favourite Chardonnay white wine.)

Step 3: Choose some extra images based on whatever creative inventions your mind conjures up. (Like *Cher and Donnie* or *charred hay.*)

Step 4: Fix these main images into place in a memory journey. (Perhaps bottles of Chardonnay in a pile of charred hay in your back garden.)

Step 5: Attach extra images for any other details you want to remember: new facts, key words, follow-up instructions, supporting ideas. (Maybe the Eiffel Tower rising up out of the hay, reminding you of this wine's French origins.)

Keep in mind all the other principles and practices you've learnt during your training so far, and push yourself to use your memory at its brilliant best.

Tasting Wine: A Beginner's Guide

Start by using your eyes. Fill the bottom of your glass and hold it up to the light. Look carefully at the colour and clarity of the wine. The tint of every bottle is different, and with practice you can learn a great deal simply by looking at wine.

Next, search for clues with your nose. Lift your glass to your nose and smell the wine. If you lower the glass for a moment, hold it by the stem and rotate it for a few seconds: the swirling wine will be oxygenated and release even more flavour. Note any smells you detect: fruity, woody, smoky, leathery …?

Now it's time to examine the wine with your tongue. Start with a small sip and move the liquid around your mouth. This helps to cleanse your palate for the full taste to come. Take the second sip more slowly and swish the wine in your mouth to extract the full flavour. Make a note of all the tastes you can pick out.

When you're ready, close your eyes and explore the information you've just installed in your mind. If you want to learn more, you'll find there's space here to add as much extra detail as you want – but even this short text should have given you some useful starting skills, because you knew how to make the most of every word you read.

Now have a go at writing down everything you learnt about wine tasting, talking about it to someone from memory, or even putting it into practice at a real wine-tasting event.

---

brilliant impact

This is remembering at its best – and it keeps getting better. Every time you walk back through a memory journey and engage with the information, you alter it slightly and heighten the memory. And even if you haven't gone back for a while, the main images will still be there, and the smaller details can be quickly refreshed. You're not starting from scratch every time you rehearse or revise: you're strengthening and extending memories that have been built to last.

You'll be using this strategy when you learn how to speak from memory, and again when you explore the ultimate approach to exams. But for now, take every opportunity you get to practise it in real life: with newspaper features, web-pages, research notes, science guides, history leaflets. See how much more you remember, and how much more you can *do* with it all, when you know how get the best out of your brain.

Language learning

When you can manipulate words in your mind and make them memorable, you can boost your confidence with language in general, improving your spelling, widening your vocabulary and giving you a whole new approach to learning whole new languages.

Spellings

General advice

As always, the process starts with a decision to do more than just hope for the best. Take an active approach and start making every spelling powerfully memorable.

- Highlight difficult details in bold colours in your mind.
- Exaggerate the easy-to-miss bits: make tricky letters huge, 3D, moving ... whatever makes them stand out.
- Take a mental photograph to imprint every customised word on your brain.
- Hold your paper high and look up at the spellings. This matches your upwards eye-movements when remembering words; and most people seem to find it easiest to look up *left* to learn spellings, because that's where they look in their mind to find them again.
- Practise re-creating the word in your mind's eye – and make sure it's there securely by spelling it backwards.
- Write out spellings on paper to build up muscle memories.

Targeted techniques

You can also make yourself very precise memory triggers for the words you always get wrong. Often you only need to remember one small detail to get the spelling right every time.

Double/single letters

To remember the double letters in *address*, why not picture Donald Duck (DD) and Steven Spielberg (SS) living at the same address? See it in your mind's eye and use this image whenever the word *address* crops up.

To remember that there's only one *t* in the middle of *commitment*, you could imagine someone showing complete commitment to the *IT* department at work.

Silent letters

If you were having problems with the silent *h* in *character*, you might focus on the word *char* that's visible when it's spelt right. You could then decide to get a match and *char* a picture of every character in a particular book or TV show; or even just give them a *chair* to sit on. And don't just think about it, push yourself to *see* it. With this active approach you can start imprinting very strong image-clues about all the spelling details you find difficult.

There's an easy-to-miss *i* in *miniature*, so why not imagine a miniature pottery figure coming to life and stuttering 'I … I … I …'; or go one step further and make it a miniature *eye*.

Tricky vowels

Is it *relevant* or *relavent*, *seperate* or *separate*?

You might spot the girl's name *Eva* in the correct spelling of *relevant*: maybe the office assistant who helps you to find the relevant paperwork.

How could you *separate* two golfers who *par* every hole on the course?

brilliant tip

Always be on the look-out for words-within-words (when they're spelt properly), familiar initials, names, anagrams, patterns … anything that gives your memory something to hold on to – especially if it suggests useful images to fix the tricky bits in your mind. It's a very practical approach because it exercises your eye for detail and your ability to spot spelling patterns, as well as filling in particular gaps in your knowledge. Picture yourself trying to *tell* an *intellectual* he's wrong; *building* a sink with an oversized *U*-bend; thinking up an *eg* of every possible *category* of spelling …

Memory sentences

For longer or more unusual spellings, memory sentences can be your best bet. I still remember how to spell *beautiful* because I was told in infant school that Big Elephants Are Useful To Indians For Unloading Logs, because … the initial letters spell out the tricky word. This technique isn't foolproof so use it sparingly – and carefully.

brilliant tip

- Write memory sentences with exactly the right number of words. 'Rhythm Helps You To Hear Music' is better than '(I'm) Really Hoping (That) You'll Teach Him (The) Macarena'.

- Make your sentences memorable in their own right: interesting, appropriate, surreal, surprising … *something* that helps them to stick. 'Your Anchor Could Have Tangled' for *yacht* offers a clear picture and an intriguing problem.

- Try to find a connection with the original word. It's not always possible, and other things can just as easily remind you of the sentence you need: for example, I remember the elephants, Indians and logs by picturing the teacher who told me about them. But it can be a useful trigger for your memory if the theme of the sentence matches the word in question: 'Egyptians Give You Pyramid Tours', for instance, for *Egypt*.

> ● Practise saying the sentences and get used to how they sound. It's a bit like the muscle memories you build up for movements with your hands or feet: you get used to the feel of the words as you say them aloud. If I tried saying 'Big elephants *help* Indians …' I'd spot the change in rhythm immediately and know something had gone wrong.

Vocabulary

Which one is it?

There are some confusing pairs of words that look or sound the same but have very different meanings and uses. Your new attention to detail and understanding of memory will help you set up useful reminders about which is which.

Desert/dessert

In the desert there's only sand, and *desert* has only one *s*; but in a *dessert* there could be lots of things beginning with *s*: sugar, strawberries, suet, semolina, syrup … Use imagery to help you see the clear contrast between two very similar words.

Principal/principle

If your school Principal was called Al, and you pictured him with Al written on his door and saw him wearing a name-badge saying Al, you'd remember that a *Principal* is usually a person – unlike a *principle* which is always just an idea.

Stationary/stationery

Picture the *stationer*, the person who sells you your *stationery* supplies. Imagine what they might be holding or doing and create a memorable image of the *stationer* – to remind you of *stationery*.

Memorable meanings

You can also set up images to link individual words to their specific meanings. You play around with letters and sounds, find new ideas to turn into memorable pictures, then connect those pictures to the real meanings you need to know. There are several steps involved but soon you'll be doing them almost without thinking. It's active, energetic learning – but it feels right because it suits the way your memory works. It's particularly powerful when you want to remember unusual vocabulary, like …

Agelast: a person who never laughs

You might split this word into two: *age* and *last*. If you never laugh, maybe you *age last* because your face doesn't get any laughter lines. Picture the smooth, unlined skin of any *agelast* you know …

Agrestic: rude or coarse

How about combining *aggressive* with *tic* – one of those annoying little parasites you can pick up in the woods. Visualise, personalise and exaggerate … by picturing a particularly *aggressive tic* being rude to you and using the coarsest language you've ever heard.

Rugate: wrinkled

Remember that *rug* you *ate*? Think about how wrinkled it was, how the wrinkles felt as you ate them, and how you wrinkled up your face in disgust.

Logophile: a lover of words

A useful play on words here might be 'logger file': the cardboard file that all loggers keep containing all the words they love about trees …

Foreign vocabulary

Here are examples from German, French and Spanish, but this strategy works with any language you want to learn. In practice you'll always have many more clues to help you – like links with other words, familiar spelling patterns, and of course all the words that don't change much or at all between languages. But this exercise should prove that any word or phrase, even if it's been taken completely out of context, can be memorised brilliantly.

In each list of random words and phrases below, use the ready-made imagery to learn the first five items, then have a go at memorising the next five yourself.

brilliant tip

Remember, you don't need to invent images to represent the whole of a word: just think up 'bridging' pictures that get you close enough to the right sound or spelling. Find words-within-words, pick out key syllables, extract associations based on the way a word looks or sounds – and then, if you connect those images to the real meaning, your brain will always have a way of bridging the language gap.

German

Das Bett: bed
Maybe you have to win a *bet* at the miniature casino on your pillow before you're allowed to come to bed.

Zu Fuss: on foot
Everywhere you walk on foot there are zebras, lions, tigers and monkeys causing chaos – a '*zoo fuss*'.

Der Abend: evening
Do *a bend* to exercise your back every evening.

Die Mutter: mother
How she likes to *mutter*! Hear her mutterings echoing in your head.

Rot: red
Every red thing is starting to look and smell like it's starting to *rot* ...

Die Birne: pear

Das Hemd: shirt

Der Kiefer: jaw

Das Becken: basin

Guten Tag: hello

French

L'armoire: wardrobe
What if you found that a spooky old suit of *armour* was now the only thing hanging in your wardrobe?

La tasse: cup
Imagine the look and feel of a French cup covered in *tassels*.

Le traiteur: deli
How do you know the woman behind the deli counter is a *traitor*?

Le pain: bread
Feel the searing *pain* as you bite into a slice of French bread.

Le chou: cabbage
Imagine finding something green and leafy inside your *shoe* ...

La carte: map

Le lait: milk

Merci: thank you

Blanc: white

Le loup: wolf

Spanish

El pollo: chicken
What would a *polo*-playing chicken look like?

El tenedor: fork
Use your fork to prise a *tenner* off the *door*.

La cartera: schoolbag
If your schoolbag turned into a '*car-tearer*', what level of destruction might it wreak?

La lucha libre: wrestling
Picture yourself eating *lunch* in the *library* and watching the other readers wrestle.

El camarero: waiter
Imagine the waiter taking your photograph, but asking why the viewfinder says '*camera error*'.

Algo mas?: anything else?

Rosado: pink

El parpado: eyelid

El horno: oven

El raton: mouse

brilliant tip

To remember the gender of foreign words, why not develop your own simple image code? Whenever you create a picture to remind you of a masculine word, you could give it a particular colour – blue, say, to contrast with feminine words painted pink. And if there are neuter words, maybe you could visualise them in various shades of grey. Alternatively you could position the images in different, well-defined areas of your imagination. Maybe you designate a particular building to hold images of all the words in a new language, and put the masculine words upstairs and the feminine ones down. Or you might visualise foreign words arranged around an entire town or city, giving you plenty of appropriate locations for all the new vocabulary – and more than enough space to have exclusive districts for masculine, feminine and neuter words.

So, to apply your memory skills to learning languages:

- decide to use your brain brilliantly
- think strategically to choose key words and phrases
- personalise the information: make it mean something to you
- visualise 'bridging' images to link new words with their familiar meanings
- exaggerate every detail
- organise your imagery to keep hold of it in your memory

... and then step seven, *practise*, is more important than ever. Memory skills install new words in your head and give you the support you need to start speaking and writing them; but it's by using them in real situations that you become fluent. Too many people never get to that stage – and quickly forget all the words and phrases they *thought* they'd learnt. But if you can use trigger images to give you the confidence to chat and shop and travel in a foreign country, *that's* when the real learning begins. Say hello in Berlin; eat a *pomme* in Paris; connect your imaginary ideas with the real things, the real experiences, the real, living language ... and you'll be making memories that last.

🔍 brilliant impact

Now that you're so good with words, why struggle to remember passwords any more? When you're choosing new passwords for computer systems, social networking sites or online accounts, simply choose ones that match the way your memory works. You can be extremely strategic by choosing the words and the image triggers to remember them *at the same time*.

So you might imagine logging on to a dating website and seeing your favourite film star appear on screen and say hello to you personally: password = bradsayshi.

You could think about the gadget you're saving up for as you log on to your bank account, and imagine yourself viewing the details *on* it at that very moment, a wide, flat screen filled with numbers: password = hugeplasmatv.

Choose passwords based on personal information that no one could guess. Focus on the details of words to remember them, but also to make them even more secure: running words together, for example, including deliberate misspellings or using made-up words that only you'd be likely to remember, thanks to your new memory skills.

To make your passwords even more secure, why not mix words with numbers?

The next chapter will show you how to develop complete confidence with numbers in every form: times, dates, prices, codes, sums … More than just coping with numbers you'll start choosing to use them, improving your success in some surprising areas and taking your brain training to new levels of brilliance. Now that you know how to handle words, you can start holding on to even more of those detailed bits of data that make such a difference to everything you do.

 recap

● Look at words like a crossword compiler and extract every memorable detail.

● Assign 'trigger images' to words, based on real meanings and free association.

● Highlight key points in a text, then add picture clues about everything else.

● Give tricky words powerful, visual reminders of how they're spelt.

● Use 'bridging' images to make links between new words and their meanings.

CHAPTER 8

Numbers and names

Do not trust your memory; it is a net full of holes; the most beautiful prizes slip through it.

Robertson Davies

In this chapter you will learn:

- a range of systems for remembering numbers
- easy ways to learn everyday digits: TV channels, times, dates, prices, PINs ...
- the skills involved in putting names to faces
- simple techniques for helping other people to remember you
- how to manage your life by linking numbers to names

You're not alone: everyone finds numbers and names hard to remember. Numbers are abstract ideas, hard to hold on to, easily confused. Names are arbitrary labels that can be too common, too rare, too complicated or just too straightforward to stay in your head. Both are often presented in the worst ways imaginable: a long phone-number called out across a busy office; five new names fired at you around a restaurant table. And both are particularly frustrating because they have such a major impact on your life.

⤴ brilliant impact

Just think – if you could cope with numbers, you'd be able to:

- remember meeting times, appointment dates, birthdays, anniversaries
- make better judgements about prices, negotiate more favourable deals

- save time making phone calls, following directions, finding addresses

- recall DIY measurements, recipe amounts, clothes sizes

- learn history dates, geography statistics, science facts, literary references

If you knew how to learn names, you could:

- strengthen your relationships with colleagues at work

- improve your networking skills and make powerful new contacts

- feel more confident in social situations

- boost your knowledge about famous figures, past and present

- make sure other people remember you for all the right reasons

And if you were brilliant with them *both*, you'd be able to bring a new level of order to every area of your life: linking people to their birthdays; connecting names and addresses, ages, phone-numbers, order references, team positions; recalling whom to meet in which office at what time …

The benefits of knowing numbers and names are clear; but so too are the dangers of forgetting them. If you've ever sent something to the wrong address, bought a piece of furniture that was just too big, missed an important appointment, forgotten a special birthday or anniversary or made a mistake about something as clear cut as someone's name … then you'll know how embarrassing, frustrating and costly it can be to let these particular 'prizes' slip through the net.

 Memory is what tells a man that his wife's birthday was yesterday.

Mario Rocco

This chapter is about getting to grips with some of the hardest-to-hold information. It will provide you with practical strategies for storing these vital details; show you how to make the most of everything else you've learnt about your memory; and give you a wide range of applications so that you can start putting your new-found confidence to use.

You can do it. You've already seen clear evidence of your memory's phenomenal power. You've proved that strategies and systems can have a revolutionary impact on your learning. Now you're ready to get your brain in gear and master numbers and names once and for all.

Numbers

Systems for remembering numbers have been around for centuries, and they all work on the same basic principle: that numbers are hard because they're intangible and abstract, so to make them easier you need to make them *mean* something. We do that naturally when we spot familiar number-facts or find patterns that suggest some sort of meaningful design. Number systems simply give you a way to do it quickly and easily every time.

Number rhymes

Rhyme has played an important role in the history of number learning. As well as individual verses, like: 'In sixteen hundred and sixty-six, London burned like rotten sticks', a very specific strategy has been around for centuries that uses rhyme to make numbers so much more memorable.

Instead of thinking of abstract ideas – 'one, two, three' – you use rhymes to give you concrete images: 'bun', 'shoe', 'tree'. These can be used as 'pegs' for other bits of information, or the images themselves can be linked into pairs or larger sets, connected to other kinds of information, organised into imaginative stories or arranged around journeys of the mind.

The Number Rhyme System is quick to learn and it delivers immediate results. It can struggle with longer lists or large sets of numbers, but it's a useful strategy to have up your sleeve, and a good way to see what happens when you turn numbers into pictures.

Start by setting up ten rhyming images. Here are some suggestions, but it's your memory, so use rhymes that are going to work for you.

1   sun, bun, gun

2   shoe, loo, goo

3   key, tree, sea

4   door, saw, war

5   hive, jive, drive

6   bricks, sticks, tricks

7   heaven, Devon, Evan

8   skate, gate, Kate

9   wine, vine, mine

10 hen, pen, wren

For digit learning you'll also need 0: so how about 'port' for *nought* or 'hero' for *zero*?

So you simply choose your favourite rhyme for each of the numbers, zero to 10. Then, whenever you want to learn a numbered list, you have a ready-made row of 'pegs' on which all the items can be hung. And to remember numbers themselves, you've got some very clear pictures to use instead.

brilliant tip

The seven steps to building strong memories still hold true. Plan what you're going to do with the images, visualise them with as much personal, powerful detail attached as possible, organise them in effective ways – and then practise with them until the memories are fixed.

Learning a list

To learn the following inventory of household objects ...

lamp   TV   bath   vase   bed   curtains   computer
dishwasher   fridge   toaster

... simply create a strong mental picture for each one and link it to the appropriate number image, using the sort of connections that form the organising structure of your memory stories. One thing can be joined to another, or transform into it, explode to release it, smash into it, play with it, eat it ... Remember to include all your senses, to imagine your own reactions to what's going on, and to exaggerate every memorable detail.

Here are some ideas:

1   *lamp:* if your rhyme for '1' was 'sun', you could imagine the lamp burning as brightly as the sun itself. If you'd chosen 'bun', you might design your lamp to look exactly like a delicious currant bun.

2   *TV:* smashing the TV with a shoe, a show about loos, or a TV-set covered in sticky goo.

3   *bath:* perhaps there's a tiny key floating in your bath, or a tree growing up through the water.

4   *vase:* open the door and knock a priceless vase to the floor, or picture the vase painted with vivid scenes of war.

5   *bed:* a tiny bed for every bee in the hive; a jive competition being held on your bed; or the bed being moved from the bedroom to sit in the middle of the drive ...

Now it's your turn. Have a go with the next five items on the list.

6   *curtains*

7   *computer*

8   *dishwasher*

9 *fridge*

10 *toaster*

When you've designed your five image links and given yourself a couple of minutes to practise, see how many of the original ten objects you can remember, using the number-rhyme 'pegs' to organise your creative ideas. Can you go through the whole list, backwards as well as forwards? What was the eighth item? What came before the curtains?

---

brilliant timesaver

Just like memory journeys, the number-rhyme system lets you use one memory to trigger another. Each image hooked on to one of the ten pegs can be the starting-point for a scene or story designed to store as much information as you like. The bun-shaped lamp might fall over into a luxurious chocolate cake and have to be prised out with a long stick of celery. After being smashed by your shoe, what if the TV set started leaking litres of coffee on to the carpet – with juicy green olives floating in it? The key could be floating in a bath full of strawberry jam, and a passing chicken might get its feet stuck … until it pulled on a long sausage and dragged itself free – only to fall into a huge pot of sugar … Suddenly, '3' isn't just *bath*, it's also *strawberry jam, chicken, sugar* … and you've got a detailed shopping list that you won't forget in a hurry!

Learning numbers

Your friend's new house number is 48, so you might imagine them holding a *saw* with a pair of *skates* hanging from the end.

Rob's extension number is 72, so you could visualise a *heavenly shoe* sitting on his desk: bright white, decorated with angels and haloes.

Your top price in the negotiations is £56,000, so perhaps you imagine hitting a hive with sticks, releasing the bees, being stung … and the pictures in your mind would help you to avoid being stung for real.

Have a go yourself. Check you have ten images based on number rhymes, then use them to learn the following facts.

You need to go to a meeting in room 39.

The security code on your bank card is 924.

The prize is behind door number 6.

Your hotel room is 1875.

Your favourite TV show is starting now on channel 606.

brilliant tip

Sometimes the basic pictures will work fine, but you can always be creative about the way you interpret the rhymes. The number 7 starts as 'heaven', but it might also be 'heavenly', 'heaven-sent', angels, haloes, fluffy clouds … The number 2 could be any kind of footwear. Zero might turn into the super-hero of your choice, a costume or gadget – or even one of his special powers. So 720 could be an angel wearing shoes decorated with pictures of Superman, a cloud holding up a ballet shoe and a utility belt, or a heavenly shoemaker leaping between tall buildings.

Did you know?

With a bit of creative thinking you can write sentences that represent long sequences of numbers. There's a technique called the *Word Length System* in which you simply choose words with particular numbers of letters, then weave them into memorable

> sentences and stories. Zero is a bit of a problem, but you can solve it by using a ten-letter word or including some other agreed detail – maybe just a word beginning with z. To learn the serial number on your bike, 45597, you might use a memorable phrase like: 'lock every night, defeating thieves'. 'Contains my precious yesterdays' could be how you remember the combination lock on your secret diary: 8280.

The Major System

French mathematician and astronomer Pierre Herigone invented this memory system back in the 1600s, but it's been developed over the centuries and used by people all around the world. The idea is that each digit is represented by a designated consonant or consonants, which can be turned into words and phrases by including the vowels of your choice. And once you've got meaningful words to work with, rather than tricky, abstract numbers, the rest of your memory skills can do their thing.

The most common version of the Major System looks like this:

0: *s*, *z* or soft *c*: *z* is the first letter of the word 'zero', and the other consonants here sound similar.

1: *d* or *t*: like the number 1, these letters both have one downstroke.

2: *n*: like 2, it has two downstrokes.

3: *m*: this time both the number and its letter have three downstrokes.

4: *r*: the last letter of 'four'; and 4 and R are almost mirror images.

5: *l*: in the system of Romal numerals, L stands for 50.

6: *j*, *sh*, soft *ch*, *dg*, *zh* and soft *g*: a handwritten *j* looks like a 6 – and *g* like a 6 upside down.

7: *k*, hard *c*, hard *g*, hard *ch*, *q* or *qu*: there are two 7s in a K.

8: *f* or *v*: a handwritten *f* looks like an 8, and *v* sounds similar.

9: *b* or *p*: *b* looks like 9 rotated, *p* could be a mirror-image 9, and the two letters have a similar sound.

The Major System is phonetic: sound-based. Spellings don't matter because it's the consonant sounds of a word that give you its number code.

So the number 974190 could be learnt as BiG ReD BuS.

Castle holds the numbers 705 (CaSL).

To remember that your car is parked in bay 31 you might picture it covered in MuD.

To learn the first eight digits of *Pi*, you could use the Major System to give you MeTeoR TaiL PiNK: 3.1415927.

---

brilliant tip

Don't get confused by double letters. The real word you've chosen may need them to be spelt correctly, but if they make one sound they should only represent one number. For example, the word *bliss* would be used to remember 950, not 9500. For 9500, *blue seas* would work perfectly. *Kill* is 75, not 755; but 755 could be *Kill Lee*.

The Major System takes a bit of learning but it's a very powerful way of memorising specific numbers, allowing you to create strong images and to connect them directly to your subject matter. It can be a bit complicated and time consuming for everyday number learning, but it's great for longer numbers – especially the ones you want to learn long term.

To see if the Major System might work for you, try using it to memorise the following information.

Remember the key steps:

● Turn each digit into a consonant from the list.

● Group the consonants into real words, inserting vowels as necessary.

● Create strong images for the words you've chosen.

● Find ways to link these images with the numbers you started with.

Your new fridge can't be wider than 67 cm.

The antique vase was made in 1743.

Your mother-in-law's birthday is 24/11.

The catalogue code for your new television is 349658302.

And what about the other way round? See how quickly you can change the following images back into the numbers that count.

Every time you press the buttons on the security door at work, you imagine hearing an EVIL LION. So, what's the code?

Think what would happen if you had NO PROOF that your credit card actually belonged to you. What's your PIN?

When you want to phone your friend Alice, you think about her wearing an OLD BLUE SHEET – so what's her number?

(The answers, by the way, are 8552, 2948 and 519561.)

🌐 **brilliant** timesaver

If you need to remember lots of two-digit numbers (like birth years, Bingo calls, football squad numbers) or long number sequences, it's a good idea to invest some time in developing your own double-digit system. You could easily use the Major System's number/letter combinations to turn every two-digit number into a familiar person, giving you a powerful, ready-made image for every pair of numbers, and instantly cutting your workload in half.

You might decide to turn 00 into Steven Spielberg

01 could be Sammy Davis Jr

19: Tweety Pie

36: Michael Jackson

64: Julia Roberts

77: King Kong

It's great memory training to design and rehearse your own system and then put it into practice, turning pairs of numbers into people that can be incorporated in any of your other memory techniques.

Number shapes

This strategy is popular because it's easy to remember the key images, but they can all be extended to provide a wide range of possibilities.

Each of the ten digits has a main image based on the way it looks. Here's one set of ideas, but you can easily customise it to suit the way you see numbers – as long as each image is different from all the others.

0 looks like a ball

1 is the same shape as a pencil

2 could be a swan

3 on its side resembles hills

4 might suggest the sail on a yacht

5 looks like a sharp hook

6 tipped forward might be a cannon

7 resembles a lamp

8 could be a snowman

9 looks like a lollipop

You can use these ready-made images for remembering straight-forward information like:

House numbers
Picturing a swan sitting on your aunt's doorstep holding a pencil in its beak would remind you that she lives at number 21.

Measurements
Seeing a snowman sailing a boat across your kitchen table would remind you that it's 84 cm wide.

Statistics
Imagining a cannon on the banks of the Amazon shooting doves over snowmen playing football … would tell you that this river's length is 6280 km.

You can also expand the main images to give you more options. As well as being a ball, 0 could be any kind of sporting equipment: golf club, tennis racket, bike helmet. For 3 you could go beyond hills to think about anything in the countryside: trees, flowers, rabbits. The number 6 could be more sorts of weaponry than just a cannon: crossbow, slingshot, atomic bomb … Just make sure that any extra ideas you pick are clearly connected to a number's main 'theme'.

brilliant tip

For longer sequences of numbers, make it easier to write memory stories by including verbs and adjectives as well as nouns.
With practice you can create concentrated stores of detailed information.

- The number 2 could be a bird, aeroplane or kite – or the action of flying, floating or gliding.
- You might want to visualise 7 as a lamp, torch or candle – or 'bright', 'shiny' or 'hot'.
- If you needed to know the security code 2170674, you could tell yourself a story about a penguin (2) writing (1) on a glowing (7) golfball (0) and then firing it (6) into the hot (7) sea (4). Stretch your creative brain and start turning numbers into the most varied, rich and memorable stories imaginable.

When you know how to handle numbers, you can add them to other collections of information.

Improve your passwords

Make your passwords more secure by inserting seemingly random numbers. If you've chosen the password *myfriends* for your social networking website, and you're already used to visualising a group picture of your friends on the computer screen, you could now imagine the person on the left holding a beachball (0) and the one on the right trying to spike it with a hook (5). Now your password is 0myfriends5: much safer!

Add extra detail to your life planning

Remember the to-do list you learnt in Chapter 5? Rather than just remembering to go to the bank, you could now leave yourself a reminder to withdraw £40 (a wet tennis ball on the bank teller's desk) from account number 7523 (a glowing hook stuck into a floating tree in the lobby). You've already got multi-layered imagery to remind you about Scott's birthday card, and now you can include a reminder about his address (a lollipop (9) and a rose (3) sticking out of the model castle on the card). He lives at 93 Castle Street.

Personal numbers

Lots of other numbers you need to know – birthdays, phone extensions, team numbers – are linked to people; so, to learn them, you need sound strategies for remembering names. And names are a very powerful example of the complexities of memory. The names you know well are some of the easiest things to recall, but new names can be hard to hold in your head even for a few seconds. Your right brain helps you to recognise faces you've seen before; your left brain should lead you to the details of their name; but bringing the two sides together – often under time pressure and amidst a range of distractions – can be frustratingly hard.

Did you know?

Context is particularly significant when you're trying to remember names. Memory relies a great deal on expectation. You know you're likely to meet your colleague Sarah in the corridors at work, but when you bump into her in the middle of town it's so much harder to remember who she is, let alone what she's called. We also expect people to *look* a certain way – so any changes in hairstyle or clothing can play havoc with our memory. It's one of the reasons why people are so hard to remember: they change location and appearance, and your natural memory needs lots of artificial help.

Expecting to forget

Another reason why names are so tricky is that we try to learn them in the worst possible conditions. Your memory training should have shown you the importance of taking control: deciding to use your memory well, making a clear plan about how to do it, and utilising your whole brain to fix information firmly in your mind. But when it comes to learning names, all too often we:

- assume it's going be impossible
- do nothing to improve the quality of the information that's given to us
- rely on nothing more than our natural recall

No wonder names prove to be such a problem.

The solution is contained in the seven steps of memory making. Now more than ever you need clear strategies for taking charge of challenging situations, and active learning techniques to get your brain working brilliantly.

Remembering names

Step 1: Deciding

You have to assume that you're going to remember the names you come across and the people you meet: not just by trying harder, but by doing it better. You need to concentrate from the start and put in the right sort of effort – and you need to prepare yourself to find the space and time to do it properly. Going into any name-learning situation, you've got to be very clear about what you want to get out of it, and what you're going to do to make your memory work.

Step 2: Strategising

Your strategy for success needs to kick in the moment you hear someone's name – because, unless you listen carefully, your memory really doesn't stand a chance. It's hard enough to stop and focus on the names we read, but in real-life situations they're often fired at us so quickly or quietly or while we're so busy shaking hands or thinking of something to say that they're extremely hard to take in. At business events or on social occasions there are usually numerous other distractions, too: in the room around us, but also *within* us – nerves, excitement, our eagerness to please ... Even when we're just reading names in a document our brains are often too busy with other things to take much notice. So the first stage of remembering people has to be looking and listening, concentrating on a name, actively taking it on board and starting to do something with it. It's an area of learning where we can often be extremely strategic, choosing exactly whom to remember – and *how*.

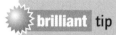 **brilliant** tip

Be interested in names, ask how they're spelt, what they mean. Repeat them immediately: 'Hello Chris, really nice to meet you.' Hear the name, look at the person, and tell yourself that you're going to put together a memory that will last.

Step 3: Personalising

Some of the things that make name learning hard – like the emotional strains involved in meeting people – can be turned round and used to your advantage. As you meet someone new, consciously consider how you feel. Say their name in your head as you think: do I like this person? Are they attractive? Is what they're saying interesting? Would they make a good colleague, friend, partner ...? Set up connections through feelings and you're much more likely to recall the meeting, but you'll also be creating mental links to their name – especially when you focus on what the moment 'means', and on your reasons to remember.

Step 4: Visualising

As well as looking at the person in front of you, look at their *name* – in your mind's eye. Picture it written across their face or picked out in a neon sign hanging above their head. Imagine what their signature might look like. Whether you're reading a name on paper or seeing it in your head, treat it just as you would any other word: as a collection of letters and sounds that can provide you with memorable possibilities. What does the name sound like or look like? Do particular syllables suggest objects, people, places? Are there words-within-words that could give you useful associations? Unpick names to reveal images that you can work with. For example:

Harry Floris

Harry looks and sounds like *hairy*. Floris is very similar to *florid*, red-faced; and to *florist*, a flower-seller. The first syllable of his surname sounds like *floor*, but it also looks like *flow*. *Flow rice?* Rice flowing across the floor? The name Flo is in there, along with Lori – and Rolf, backwards: perhaps the people being swept away by the flow ...?

Angela MacDonald

There's an *angel* in Angela, maybe one with *gel* in its hair. The *Mac* could be a raincoat. Donald might get you thinking of Donald Duck, or another famous Don: Johnson, Quixote, Corleone ...

Step 5: Exaggerating

As soon as you've extracted some image ideas, make them important. Imagine they're part of this moment, revealing key aspects about this person in front of you and providing you with big clues about who they are. Ask yourself questions and exaggerate the answers – along with everything else that you start seeing in your mind's eye.

- Why is this red-faced man taking his flowery shirt off so flamboyantly? To show you his hairy chest. The hairs reach to the floor, which also seems to be covered in rice, flowing around you and hairy Harry Floris.

- Why has this woman got a halo hanging over her gelled-back hair? Imagine she's holding a mac that seems to be wrapped around a writhing, quacking duck. Clearly Angela MacDonald has a very famous character in her heavenly raincoat! As always, make the imagery bold and bright, funny, strange, violent, surprising – and powerfully memorable.

Step 6: Organising

On paper or in person, names need to be connected to their owners. You've already started this process by using your feelings about them, picturing their names imprinted on them and visualising strange and memorable things happening *to* them. Even just reading the name of a party host or conference delegate should get you linking imagery with a real character – even one you've never actually seen.

brilliant tip

If you're learning names on paper, connect the images you create to what the real person *could* look like or might be expected to do.

- Your new colleague is called Fred Bloom. Imagine him walking into your office wearing bright red clothes and carrying a bunch of *bloo*ming flowers. Maybe he's half red, half blue (for *Bloom*). Why does he seem so worried about finding the *loo*? As he sits down at his desk, why is he setting up a *loom*?

- If you learnt that Henry the Eighth's first wife was called Catherine of Aragon, you could imagine her doing something with a *cat* and a *rag*, being *arrogant*, getting into *a rage* ... put her into a scene alongside her infamous husband ... and set up memorable images even before you found out anything more about her.

But when you've got the real person in front of you there's so much more you can do to connect them with their name. As well as seeing them act out the images you've designed, you can use the way they look and the things they're wearing to help you.

Lookalikes

Does this person remind you of someone else? It could be a famous face or a family member, but it makes sense to use any resemblance they have to someone you already know. What if they were really that other person in disguise? How would that make you feel, and how might it change the things you imagine?

- If your new neighbour Andy Webster happens to look like Elvis, you could imagine him using his huge hands (Andy) to *stir* the *webs* (Webster) on his garden fence – dressed in a Las Vegas jumpsuit and gyrating his hips like the King. When you next bumped into him, you'd have the Elvis connection to take you straight to the images based on his name. You'd still be able to get there by picturing him standing by his fence, and you'd still have the 'fake' recollection of how you felt when you saw his cleaning and dancing in action; but you'd also be using his physical appearance as a direct link into your multi-layered memory for *Andy Webster*.

- Maybe your colleague Helen Martino looks like the Queen of England. Imagine this really *is* the Queen in disguise, arriving at your office in a royal limousine decorated with devils and fiery furnaces (images of *hell* for Helen) and drinking from a huge Martini cocktail (Martino). Look for clues in the jewellery she's wearing (are those miniature crowns on her necklace?) or in the way she walks (like she's in a regal parade?) that will remind you of the royal connection. Even away from the context of your office her appearance should trigger you to think about a very memorable mental scene: this Queen lookalike in a hellish car drinking Martinis ... *Helen Martino*.

> ### ☀ brilliant tip
>
> Don't forget how important location is to memory. If you're ever struggling to remember the name of someone you've met, think carefully about where you were when you last saw them. Focus on the exact part of the room, building or town; see the two of you standing there; but also imagine what you could see *from* that spot, using every available detail to reconnect you with the memory.

Features and fashions

Like a caricaturist painting an exaggerated portrait, highlight any details that you could emphasise in your memory and use as links to someone's name. Temporary 'hooks' might be details of clothing, jewellery, make-up or hairstyle; but you can find more permanent links in face-shape, nose-size, birth-marks, height – anything that you'd be sure to notice about the person in question when you met them again.

- If Amira Khan had a very round face, you could imagine her looking at herself in a very round *mirror* (Amira) made out of tin *cans* (Khan).

- If Rick Carpenter was particularly tall, you might imagine him using his carpentry skills to build an incredibly high wooden shelf to hold all his model rickshaws.

Step 7: Practising

You need to start practising new names straight away, while the real person's still there in front of you. Make sure you drop their name into conversation a few times, but you can also be saying it 'aloud' in your own head, getting used to how it sounds and building up the association with its owner. At the same time you'll be creating the images and links that will keep this person in your mind for the long term; so, while you're talking to them, run through the triggers you've set up and practise following the images and associations that take you back to their name.

⤢ brilliant exercise

Try out these techniques for yourself on the following names.

With this first set, practise creating memorable images and connecting them to the people in question.

Your travel agent is Doug Reddy.

The party is being hosted by Maddie Tan.

Your new neighbours are Bart and Sue White.

With the next group of names, create images for them all and then fix them into the first five *loci* of a memory journey.

Lily Sato   Jake Moody   Rowan Carter   Imogen Fox   Carlo Mancini

---

Put these strategies into practice in your everyday life and see what a difference they make. If you follow the steps carefully, you'll start remembering people for long enough to do something more permanent with their names: putting them in your diary, adding them to your phonebook or filing them mentally in stories and journeys.

And because you know how name learning works, you can start activating memories about *you*.

✷ brilliant tip

To give other people the best chance of remembering you ...

● Introduce yourself clearly – and make sure they've heard.

- Help them to visualise your name by mentioning how it's spelt or what it means.
- Give them information about you that's easy to picture.
- Talk about logical details and imaginative ideas to activate both sides of their brain.
- Give people reasons to remember you. What's in it for them to learn your name?
- Back up their natural memory with business cards, thankyou letters or follow-up emails.

In the next chapter you'll learn more about using memory techniques to affect other people's memories: writing unforgettable exam answers, giving powerful presentations, making the best possible impact in interviews. But first, to round off Chapter 8 ...

Names with numbers

It's time to bring together the two main themes of this chapter: connecting names to numbers. This skill will also feature in many of the high-pressure memory challenges to come; but for now, you need to see how easy it is to link numbers to names.

Carol Wu lives in apartment 702.

Imagine a carol singer trying to woo Carol Woo at her apartment. She has nothing to wear for a date – until a heavenly hero gives her some beautiful shoes. In the Number Rhyme System, heaven/hero/shoe = 702.

Leon Morales' date of birth is 23.06.71.

Perhaps you picture a lion (Leon) shouting for 'more ales' (Morales) at Leon Morales' birthday party, wearing a gnome's jacket (because, in the Major System, NoMeS JaKeT = 230671) There's plenty going on in this scene, but every detail is clear – and memorable, when you put all your training into action.

Use everything you know about memory – and both sides of your brilliant brain – to remember that ...

Tom Fischer's extension number is 849.

Holly Santos owes you £458.

Rocky Singh has ordered 26 TVs and 15 DVD players.

Lola O'Neil was born on 15.09.78.

... then cover up the information and test your brilliant memory for numbers and names.

 brilliant recap

- Abstract numbers and names are easy to forget – but can be *made* memorable.

- Number systems let you turn digits into images and fix them in your mind.

- To remember people, create powerful links between names and faces.

- Use your memory training to help other people remember you.

- Link numbers and names to store key details about all the people in your life.

CHAPTER 9

Under pressure

The existence of forgetting has never been proved. We only know that some things don't come to mind when we want them.

Friedrich Nietzsche

In this chapter you will learn:

- that imagination can help you relax and focus, ready for big tests of memory
- the importance of boosting interest and attention when you're preparing for exams
- effective memory techniques for key subject areas
- how to speak from memory – and make everything you say memorable
- emergency tactics for memory chasing under pressure

It's time to focus on those moments in life when your memory really is put to the test. Some of them are planned, even chosen: exams, job interviews, audition pieces. Others come out of the blue, but still push your memory to the limits: giving witness testimony, finding an important possession that's been lost, straining your brain to remember your PIN before the ATM swallows your cash-card ... Pressure makes things much harder – which is why you need a trained brain to perform brilliantly, whether you were expecting the memory challenge or not.

Did you know?

Stress makes us activate our most primal memories, our survival instincts, rather than the thinking skills we really need to succeed. Nerves about that make-or-break business presentation, your starring role in a play or a final university exam can trigger deeply ingrained fight-or-flight responses, making your muscles twitch and your heart race and your sweat flow, but channelling energy *away* from the parts of the brain involved in recalling the specific information you need. It's why off-by-heart learning often fails completely under pressure, and why you really do need to have strong, artificial memory supports in place, ready for the times when your brain is jettisoning knowledge for action and needs something, *anything*, to hold on to.

Calm and collected

Although your imagination can quickly run away with itself and ramp up the pressure with prophecies of doom, you can learn to use your creative thinking to calm everything down. When you're preparing for any mental challenge, it's a good idea to take conscious control of your imagination and get into the right frame of mind for success. Think about the task at hand, but focus on it in the most positive way possible. You know how to create detailed, exaggerated, memorable pictures – so paint some that will help you feel good about the challenges ahead.

There are three questions to answer.

What's in it for you?

Focus ... on all the good things that will come from doing well: the new job, the place at college, entertaining your audience, getting your driving licence. Start with ideas but quickly turn them into *pictures*: your luxurious new office; meeting friends in the college bar; the loud applause as you finish your speech; taking the kids on holiday – with you at the wheel. Use all your trained powers of imagination, activate both sides of your brain, and concentrate on the *feelings* generated by seeing these positive pictures. Build happy 'memories' that will motivate you to achieve these things for real.

How will you be brilliant?

Focus ... on the way you're going to achieve your goals. See yourself taking control of the memory process, setting up the most effective conditions for learning and doing all the right things with your brain. Use your imagination to take you inside your own head, where you can picture the two sides of your brain being brought together in precisely organised and richly creative memory making. Rehearse everything involved in putting your brilliant memory into action.

Where can you go to get ready?

Focus ... on the state of mind that will maximise your memory. With your motivation clear and your strategy sorted, use your trained visualisation skills to calm your nerves and leave you feeling focused and confident. Choose a real place where you always feel relaxed, or invent somewhere perfect, and take yourself there in your mind's eye. You know how to activate all your senses, so use them to immerse yourself in the sights, sounds, textures, tastes and smells that say peace and calm. Put yourself in your comfiest armchair, smelling and tasting hot cocoa, hearing classical music; or escape to a desert island beach where you can feel the sun on your skin, hear the birds, smell the salt in the sea ... Use these imaginary experiences to counter-balance any negative pictures your mind offers up, and enjoy the way you can regulate your breathing, steady your heartbeat, and fill yourself with the calm confidence you're going to need to perform under pressure.

brilliant tip

Whenever you visit this imaginary 'confidence zone', to prepare yourself mentally for a memory challenge, squeeze your thumb and index finger together. As well as being an appropriate symbol of perfection, it acts as a physical trigger – so that, the next time you need to draw on those positive feelings, repeating the physical action will help you to repeat the mental journey.

Tests and exams

It's particularly important to ask yourself those three questions and to paint the most useful mental pictures when you're starting to prepare for an exam – and again just before you sit the paper or take the practical test. But most exams require you to maintain the right frame of mind all the way through a lengthy revision period, so there are some other useful tactics to help you boost two key elements of your success: *interest* and *attention*.

Interest

It's simply easier to remember things you're interested in.

Did you know?

A group of African tribesmen proved to have very normal memory powers for most things – apart from information about buying and selling cattle, which was a hugely important aspect of their lives. Questioned about cattle deals they'd done, they could remember the details with remarkable accuracy – because they were interested in the information and motivated to keep it fresh and accessible in their minds.

Too often we try to revise information that doesn't interest us. We all have to study some subjects that we don't immediately engage with, however strong our motivation is to do well. The trick is knowing how to *make* the material more interesting, and then keeping it that way.

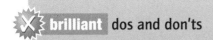 **dos and don'ts**

To boost your interest while preparing for exams:

✔ *Do ... everything you can to maintain your motivation.* As well as your positive mental pictures, find inspirational images and quotations that you can pin to your fridge or use as your screensaver. Give yourself regular 'wins' to keep you interested: little treats for achieving interim targets and reaching key points in your revision plan.

✘ *Don't ... try to learn things that you don't understand.* It's tempting to think that you're time wasting if you have to get to grips with the meaning of your material – but it's actually an essential investment. Understanding something automatically helps you to highlight key points, engage with it personally, organise it in your mind and connect it memorably with everything you already know.

✔ *Do ... make the most of your personal reactions to the things you're learning.* Examine your opinions; debate the key ideas with yourself and others; be aware of the areas that don't inspire you and look closer to find something exciting. And when you do find a topic that particularly interests you, go with it: do more research, go deeper, learn new things that will help your memory anchor everything else.

✘ *Don't ... keep going if you're not engaging with the information.* Learn to spot the times when you've lost interest and stopped connecting properly with your material – and stop. Refocus on the seven steps of memory making, especially step three: personalising. You need to know why you're doing it, what the information means to you personally and how to make it connect with you through all your senses and emotions. Revision needs to be a rich and immersive experience if it's going to work.

✔ *Do ... make your artificial memories as enjoyable and interesting as possible.* Choose images that appeal to you.

Go on memory journeys that excite you. Transform all the information you study to make it interesting and completely memorable.

Attention

Your memory training should have shown you that there's a big difference between passive and active learning, and nowhere is that more important than exam revision. It's all too easy to fool yourself that you're learning, when what you're actually doing is wasting your time. You need to direct all your attention to the task at hand – and, crucially, to how well it's going, so that you can make sure your memory is being used at its brilliant best.

brilliant dos and don'ts

To boost your attention while preparing for exams:

✗   *Don't ... fall into the trap of 'assumed learning'*. It's all too easy to think that, because you're sitting at your desk and reading your books and notes, you're learning – when actually you're only taking in the information on a very surface level. The trick is to test yourself regularly. Research shows that the testing process itself deepens memory, and it's a crucial way to make sure that your learning is working. If it is, keep going; and if it's not, you know you've got to do something different before it's too late.

✔   *Do ... everything you can to limit distractions*. Think carefully about where and when you're doing your revision. We're all different: some of us need a bit of background noise, others work best in silence. Do you concentrate best early in the morning or late at night, in the house or outside? The key thing is to be honest and do what works for you. If the learning's important and the goal's real, you need to give it your full attention.

✘ *Don't ... just tell yourself you're going to stick to your plans.* Have a practical response ready for when the going gets tough. Studies have shown the importance of being properly prepared to resist temptations and equipped to get back on track. If you're too tired to revise today, what will you do? If your friends invite you out when you'd been planning to study, how will you respond – to carry on with your normal life but also to keep focused on your goal?

✘ *Don't ... let other people get in your way.* Working with others can be extremely effective, when you help each other to understand, take turns to test and keep each other's motivation alive. But if friends or relatives are distracting you, tempting you back to bad learning habits or getting you down with their negative views, it's time to go it alone.

✔ *Do ... make the most of all your active memory skills.* Maybe you used to revise purely by reading and re-reading – and hoping ... but now you know how to take complete control of the whole learning process. Pay attention to all the details as you form your plan of attack, use your imagination to engage powerfully with your subject matter, and fix it into your mind with all the care required to remember it brilliantly.

brilliant tip

However powerful your memory skills, you need to organise your learning time effectively. Make sure you break up your revision into manageable chunks. You've seen that you naturally remember best at the start and end of every learning session, while your recall takes a dip in the middle. More, shorter sessions will make the most of the *primacy* and *recency effects*, and minimise the much weaker times in the middle. They'll also give you more mental down-time – when, in fact, your brain is sorting things out and laying down long-term memories. You'll keep your motivation strong with rest periods and little treats, but you'll be ready to get back to learning – knowing that each active memory session is taking you a step closer to your final goal.

Subject strategies

After deciding to use your memory, the strategies you set up depend a great deal on your subject matter. Your training has taught you to learn individual words, ideas, numbers and names; to store them in lists and longer collections of data; to connect them to each other flexibly; and to absorb just the right level of detail from information texts. Pick and choose from these techniques wisely – always with a clear idea about how you'll have to recall and use your learning in the final exam.

History

Preparing for a history test, you might have picked out some important dates:

1215: Magna Carta signed

1773: Boston 'tea party'

1945: UN formed

1969: First man on moon

You could easily use a number system to convert these dates into words and pictures, then learn them as a list, in a memory story or route, or combine them with other stores of information.

In the Major System, 1215 could be DNDL: a 'DoNe DeaL'.

In the Word Length System, 1773 might give you: 'a protest: dumping tea'.

For several dates in one century you could save time by inventing your own code: perhaps using one particular colour for all the images you create, linking them all to one key character or setting them all at the same appropriate location. For twentieth-century dates you might make all your images red; put Winston Churchill or Marilyn Monroe or Mickey Mouse in them somewhere; or see them all happening on the moon – since you know this was the century of the first moon landing. You can be even more precise if necessary, creating codes for decades or even individual years.

If you'd decided to link all your twentieth-century years to Mickey Mouse, you might:

- Use your personal version of the Number Rhyme System to turn 1945 into Mickey Mouse opening the door (4) of a hive (5) to find the UN gathered inside.

- Use the Number Shape system to change 1969 into Mickey Mouse sitting in a cannon (6) licking a lollipop (9) while he waits to be fired towards the moon.

Have a go yourself with three more memorable moments from the twentieth century:

1968: Martin Luther King Junior assassinated

1975: Microsoft founded

1985: Wreck of the *Titanic* discovered

brilliant tip

When you're learning from a text document – a page from a book, say, or the lecture notes you've made – use the memory journey method to help you understand the information as well as remember it.

- Reading carefully and choosing the key ideas will ensure that you know the overall themes of the material, the 'big picture'.

- Organising them into a route will help you to see patterns of ideas, the order of events and the structure of arguments.

- Designing memorable images will get you thinking even more deeply about what it all means and spotting connections within the material.

You'll understand the information better, have efficient access to the facts and ideas, be ready to use them more creatively, and take it all with you into the exam in the most memorable form imaginable.

Geography

Subjects like Geography often involve remembering names, definitions and linked facts – like the capital cities of countries around the world.

It's the same technique you use for learning languages: creating 'bridging' images to connect the pairs of words. Here you might have to play around with the names of both the country and its capital to find vivid images to bind into a memory.

The capital of Gambia is Banjul. Maybe you imagine Gambia as a *gambling* den, and every gambler inside is playing the *banjo*.

The capital of Jordan is Amman. You could picture a large statue of *a man* (a generic man, or a particular man of your choice) erected in every village and town square in Jordan – and, if you need help remembering the country, maybe every person in the crowd could look like basketball legend Michael Jordan.

Try the next three for yourself:

Country: Oman   Capital: Muscat

Country: Tuvalu   Capital: Funafuti

Country: Tanzania   Capital: Dadoma

Science

You can use creative memory techniques to store detailed scientific facts and figures.

Here's a collection of facts about acids. They:

- turn litmus paper red
- have a sour taste
- react with metals to form salts
- neutralise bases

Create a key image for 'acids' – maybe a cartoon acid barrel, fizzing and steaming menacingly – and then turn each fact into a visual detail that can be added on. A *lit mouse* (litmus) turns bright red when it's dropped into the barrel of acid. Imagine using a long, lemon-coloured straw to sip the liquid – which tastes as sour as lemon-juice. Imagine a heavy metal band playing a concert on top of the barrel, and being turned into pillars of salt. Their *bass* (base) guitars are completely *neutralised* ...

You could even start learning facts and figures from the periodic table.

Hydrogen is the chemical element with the atomic number 1. It is abbreviated to H. Hydrogen is the most abundant substance in the sun.

Your main image for hydrogen could be an H-bomb, with a glowing letter H printed on the side. Imagine poking it with a long pencil (1 in the Number Shape system) and setting off an explosion that's as bright as the sun.

Helium has the atomic number 2. Abbreviated to He, it was discovered in 1868.

Picture a helium balloon in the mouth of a swan (2) which has been sucking the gas and giving itself a very high-pitched laugh:

'he-he-he …!' When another bird tries to share the gas, the swan gives the *dove* a *shove* – because, in the Major System, dove/shove is 1868.

Try the next two yourself.

Lithium is element number 3 and is labelled Li. It has been used as a treatment for depression.

Beryllium is the element given the atomic number 4 and is abbreviated to Be. Beryllium is low in density and very stable at high temperatures, and has been put to use in many areas of the aerospace industry.

Maths

Your memory for numbers will give a big boost to your calculation skills, but you can also remember key bits of maths vocabulary, important rules and useful formulae.

In a scalene triangle, all the sides are different lengths.

Imagine a scaly monster, misshapen and irregular.

In a graph, the x axis is horizontal and the y axis vertical.

Imagine *eggs* rolling along the ground. Picture a little man sitting on the top of the graph shouting: '*Why* am I up so high …?'

The formula for calculating the area of a circle is $A = \pi r^2$.

There are many different ways that you could make this information memorable. It sounds like 'A equals pi r squared', so you might imagine your friend Andy – who's looking *hairier* (Area) than ever – on one side of some weighing scales, balanced by a perfectly square rabbit pie on the other.

Or, maybe you'd decide that the equals sign looks like a sandwich, the symbol for *Pi* a picnic table and the letter *r* a stool. You could visualise the penalty area on a football pitch and notice that someone has dropped a sandwich right in the middle. So, you set up a table and stool – but before you can sit down to eat, a tiny bird (2 in the Number Shape System) lands on the stool and starts pecking at the bread. This strange story would help you store all the specific details you need.

Literacy

You already know how to use active memory techniques to learn spellings and definitions, memorise character names and important details, and absorb all the information you need from notes, essays and text documents of every kind. But one other useful application for your creative memory skills is learning quotations, which can raise your writing to the next level and gain valuable marks in literacy exams.

The trick is to create memorable images that make the key ideas and exact words in a quotation vivid and precise.

'A pair of star-crossed lovers' (*Romeo and Juliet*)

Why not play around with the sounds and meanings of these words to give you a *pear* imprinted with the faces of Romeo and Juliet – covered in crossed-out stars? This new image could be a useful reminder in itself, added to a list of other key quotations or dropped into a memory journey about this particular play, the tragedies, or Shakespeare in general.

'My words fly up, my thoughts remain below' (*Hamlet*)

Picture Hamlet himself. As he performs one of his famous soliloquies, cartoon speech bubbles sprout wings and fly upwards, while thought bubbles remain below on the ground – where *R.E.M.* are *bellowing* out one of their greatest hits.

Here are three more famous lines from Shakespeare. Practise turning them into images that tell you everything you need to re-create them from memory.

'All the infections that the sun sucks up' (*The Tempest*)

'Journeys end in lovers meeting' (*Twelfth Night*)

'Cry "Havoc!" and let slip the dogs of war' (*Julius Caesar*)

⤴ brilliant impact

Designing memory images about the work of a famous writer helps you to see how *they* use images: how their word-pictures form patterns; which ideas are repeated or subtly changed; where the big themes intersect and overlap. And this highlights one of the major benefits of this exam approach as a whole. By exploring information with logic and imagination you don't just learn it, you understand it better, engaging with it on a much deeper level. By the time you take the exam, you know your subject matter inside out but you can also remember all your personal responses to it – and that's an important ingredient of top-level success.

Speaking from memory

Some tests and exams involve speaking as well as writing about what you know. For many people, *any* kind of speaking from memory is daunting, to say the least; but your memory training has already equipped you to do it brilliantly, however great the pressure to perform.

Did you know?

Actors learn their lines best when they focus on motivation. By understanding the ups and downs of a character's emotions and the 'shape' their experiences take throughout the play, they can learn their lines with remarkable speed and accuracy. Knowing what a character is feeling triggers memories for what they're going to say next, but many actors also find it helpful when they can match words to physical movements, and when they're standing in particular parts of the stage. In other words, it's all about emotional connection, active involvement, associations with places ... exactly the same things that make *your* memory brilliant.

Whether your speech is to an examination committee, a meeting at work or a roomful of wedding guests, you prepare for it in essentially the same way as you'd revise for a written exam. It's about turning your material into memorable images that you can fix firmly into your brain and rediscover whenever you want.

You memorise the information in just as much detail as you need. Some of it can be general ideas to discuss. Other parts might need to be precise facts and figures or perfectly worded quotations or jokes. But each element is stored securely, and all of it is instantly accessible, even under pressure.

When the time comes to speak, you can wander around the *loci* of your carefully prepared memory journey, like those great orators of old, and find all your key points in perfect order – along with plenty of extra details to bring your performance to life.

If you can speak from memory, rather than using a script, prompts or computer slides, there are many benefits:

Confidence

Even if you lose your notes, drop your cue-cards or have technical problems with your laptop, you know you'll be fine. Everything you want to say has been set up securely in your brain. You know exactly what every vivid image represents and how all the ideas flow together. You can even choose locations for your memory journeys that give you extra confidence because they're places where you feel happy and calm.

Performance

When you feel confident, you *look* confident – and your audience can have confidence in what you've got to say. Speaking from memory lets you maintain eye contact. You can now use your hands to emphasise your words rather than hold your notes or operate the computer, and your whole demeanour is different: relaxed and engaged with the audience, rather than focused on scripts and supports or distracted by technology.

Flexibility

You're no longer bound to your written notes or pile of prompt-cards, so you can speak for longer or shorter than necessary, change the order of your ideas and respond flexibly to any questions or feedback you get. The information has been set up in your brain to be easily accessible from any point. You'll probably hold back some of the details so that you have extra information for your responses at the end – and you'll know exactly where to go in your brain to get it.

Impact

Having the confidence to speak from memory immediately makes *you* more memorable. In fact your whole approach to learning helps your audience, because you give them information that's been organised into key points and arranged in a logical way: designed to suit your memory, and theirs. On top of that, many other aspects of your training will help you to communicate in ways that make your material stick in people's minds.

tip

To make your messages memorable:

- Make the most of the *primacy* and *recency effects*. The start and end of your talk are the bits your audience will remember most easily, so use those times to present the most important ideas. You'll have to work harder to make the rest of your material memorable. Including images, anecdotes and stories will help to keep people interested – and learning – all the way through.

- Engage your audience's attention as early as possible. They need to know that you're an entertaining and interesting speaker and that the things you have to say are going to be important. Get them asking questions in their heads from the start, setting themselves up to learn. The more passionate you are and the more you focus on the benefits of what you're saying, the more likely they'll be to put in the effort to remember it.

- Help people to connect personally with your ideas. What's in it for them as individuals to remember what you're saying? Appeal to their senses and emotions whenever you can, personalising the material and encouraging them to imagine themselves into the scenarios you describe. Get them using their brains: set them puzzles, ask for their opinions, stop them just listening and get them thinking and remembering.

Job interviews

The same techniques will also serve you well in job interviews. They're really just another kind of presenting from memory; and, more than ever, you need to know your stuff securely and flexibly, with all your prepared answers, ideas, facts and figures stored in a way that lets you access them instantly. You also need to be remembered for all the right reasons – so apply the tips above whenever your interviewers give you the chance. And …

brilliant tip

Just like the paper CV that you update from time to time, create a memory journey to hold all the information you need at your fingertips in an interview – and keep improving it. Your driveway might hold images about your education: school names, exam dates, qualifications earned. Perhaps the front door of your house is the *locus* for your 'other learning', including reminders about evening classes, training courses and relevant aspects of your personal development. Other zones around the journey could hold your well-rehearsed answers to typical questions; key selling-points about you; even the questions you've written to put to your interviewers at the end. Whenever you return to this memory storehouse, you'll be able to add, remove or change details, exaggerate certain ideas (perhaps as a result of feedback from previous interviews) and make sure it provides you with an up-to-date, 'artificial' memory of these very real things that you want to say. Even under intense pressure you'll never again be stuck for an answer. You'll remember to say the right things, and the *best* things.

Emergency memory

This chapter has focused mostly on times of planned memory pressure. Your brain training so far should also have prepared you to deal with everyday eventualities, setting you up to make quick decisions and form instant strategies about how to learn unexpected information. After mastering your short-term memory, you've proved how quickly you can form memorable images, link them into scenes and stories, and arrange them around strong frameworks in your mind. And the more memory buildings and journeys you design, the more confident you'll feel about taking control of information whenever and wherever it comes your way.

But what about those times when the pressure comes from *forgetting*: mislaying something valuable, getting lost on holiday, losing track of a vital experience, answer, name, number, idea …? Sometimes, the more important a memory is at that moment, the faster it seems to escape – however hard you try to chase it down. In fact, pursuing it just pushes it further out of reach.

When you're panicking about a memory, you really do need to have a clear recovery strategy. And to round off this chapter, here's some practical advice gained from the emergency services themselves.

To activate the memories of eye-witnesses, often people who've been involved in moments of high emotion and intense pressure, the police have found four memory techniques to be particularly powerful. Maybe they'll help you, the next time you're straining your brain to deliver the goods: mid-exam, presentation, interview – or struggling with a memory challenge that's come at you from nowhere. Suddenly, remembering is essential, the pressure's really on, but the key memory just won't come. So …

Re-create the conditions

It can help to go back to the scene of a crime (or the place you first had that brilliant idea or last saw your purse), either physically or in your imagination. Focus on the weather, the temperature of the room, the quality of the light. What about your emotional conditions: exactly how were you feeling at the time?

Pick one detail

Instead of struggling to remember everything, choose one thing to focus on: one detail that might just make you think of another, which could trigger a memory ... that leads your brain on through a series of associations ... until eventually you get to your target.

See it sideways

If you're going nowhere trying to picture a memory from one direction (probably your own perspective), try imagining it from someone else's point of view. What would the car crash, revision session, instant of inspiration – or the moment you put your glasses down – have looked like from above, far away or close up, or through a completely different pair of eyes?

Play it backwards

You've seen how good your memory is at following chains of events, stories, journeys – so trust in your ability to retrace your mental steps. Picture the robbers running out of the bank, and think: what happened just before that? And before *that*? Or visualise yourself getting out of your car, in the parking place that you now can't find again ... and think about the moment before that, sitting in the car, and before that, pulling into the parking bay, and ... see if your reverse journey will take you right back to the missing memory.

And when all else fails, *give up* – at least for a while. Do something to take your mind off the memory-chase. Try a different question in the exam. Ask your interviewer to come back to that subject later. Stop for a coffee, get on with the washing up ... or, better still, go off to the place of relaxation you designed at the start of this chapter. Often, when your mind is allowed space and time just to do its own thing, it works its own brand of memory magic – and the particular 'beautiful prize' that you feared was lost for ever ... comes back.

brilliant recap

- To prepare for pressure, set up a zone of calm relaxation in your imagination.

- Learn to make all your material interesting, and start giving it your full attention.

- Choose an appropriate memory strategy for every exam subject you study.

- Performing from memory makes you more confident, impressive and memorable.

- Police techniques can be the key to recapturing vital memories under pressure.

CHAPTER 10

Self-improvement

We all have our time machines. Some take us back, they're called memories. Some take us forward, they're called dreams.

Jeremy Irons

In this chapter you will learn:

- the importance of adopting the right attitude to memory, now and in the future
- why food and drink can have such an impact on your brain
- what to do, and *not* do, if your lifestyle is going to support your memory
- how improving your memory can improve your life – in some surprising ways
- strategies for putting your brilliant memory into action today

You've learnt how to have a brilliant memory. Now you need to keep it that way. This chapter is about the practical steps that will set you up for long-term success. Some are to do with your attitude, the way you approach getting older, coping with change, adapting your memory skills to new challenges. Others involve the very physical effects of things like diet, exercise and sleep: their immediate impact, and the role they'll play in all your learning to come.

It's a two-way street. Look after your memory and it will look after you. Put it to use, do everything you can to keep it healthy, and you'll discover even more benefits of remembering brilliantly. Memory skills themselves will support your success in all your current activities, challenging you to go further than ever before; but they'll also give you some very useful new tools, allowing you to tackle problem memories, conquer fears and phobias, reprogram habits of thinking and behaviour, and rehearse a whole new approach to life.

Your memory can change you on so many levels: in the past, present and future. The way you think and feel about your memory has a great deal to do with how you think and feel, full stop.

Getting older

There are lots of myths around ageing and memory, most of them variations on a theme of inevitable mental decline. Getting older means losing your mind – at key points along life's journey, and in an ongoing process of deterioration; or so most people seem to think ...

What's definitely true is that your memory changes throughout your lifetime. Children learn differently from adults. A girl of nine and an old man of ninety-nine certainly don't experience memory in the same way, and they don't have the same things happening in their heads. And there are other key times of change along the way. Teenagers (or, more accurately, parents of teenagers) often report a lack of attention and poor recall; and for women, pregnancy and the menopause seem to coincide with a drop in memory power. So we associate particular stages in life with forgetfulness, as well as experiencing the gradual ageing of the brain. Systems slow down, structures deteriorate; and yet ... somehow, the brain does amazing things. Teenagers pass their exams. Mothers-to-be multi-task. Menopausal women carry on with high-powered careers. Old age pensioners take degrees and learn new skills and keep enjoying their brilliant memories.

Your memory is always changing, but your brain has been coping with it since the womb. It has a remarkable ability to adapt and thrive.

Did you know?

Research into the impact of hormones on memory – including a recent study into so-called 'pregnancy brain' – suggests that the process may be much less clear cut than we thought. The forgetfulness many women experience could be more to do with shifts in emotion and attention than the fault of the hormones themselves. Whatever stage in life you're at, if hormones – or any other factor – are making you distracted, tired, worried, confused … is it really any surprise if your memory pays the price?

Many of the assumptions we make about older brains are also untrue. Ageing presents all our brains with a number of challenges, from without and within, but experiences vary, different aspects of memory age at different rates and in different ways, and the changes that do happen aren't always for the worse. In fact, some types of remembering could turn out to be better at seventy than when you were seven. Semantic memory, for example, especially your recall of words and their definitions, often seems to *improve* with age. And remember that packed lost-property box in your primary school!

Did you know?

Although neurons are being lost all the time, the rate of decline is minor after the age of about twenty. A more significant change involves the connections between neurons. Scientists have estimated that every ten years we experience a 10 per cent reduction in the length of our *axons*, the tiny projections that conduct electrical impulses from one brain cell to another. But while ageing attacks connective thinking, recent research into the 'plasticity' of the brain suggests that some of its most important mechanisms can still be strengthened if they're used well.

So it's certainly not as simple as saying that your memory gets worse as you get older. Memory changes – and you need to learn to change with it.

 Mark Twain said: '*Age is an issue of mind over matter. If you don't mind, it doesn't matter.*'

Attitude

The important thing is to have the right attitude to your changing brain. At different times of life, some aspects of memory may well become more of a challenge, but there's plenty you can do to keep your brain in shape and continue to enjoy its power. Don't believe all the negative things you might have read or heard. Remember: brilliant memory is something you *do*, rather than something you own. Teenagers often struggle to remember – but how much is that down to general anxiety, changing priorities, poor diet, lack of sleep …? You need to keep doing the right things, but also adapt to circumstances as they change. Keep an open mind, be honest about your experiences, and take every opportunity to get more out of your memory, whatever point in life you're at.

The effects of age on memory are complex. If your short-term memory is feeling weaker, but distant recollections still seem strong, how much is that simply down to *practice*: getting out of practice at quick-fire recall as the demands of life are reduced, and spending more time rehearsing precious memories of the past? Your overall mental and physical health has a huge impact on your memory, so anything stopping you feeling 100 per cent will inevitably take its toll. And remember the importance of expectation, connection, interest, attention …? If you're less motivated to remember and do fewer of the things that make your learning work, is it any wonder if your memory seems to be giving up?

brilliant definition

Senile dementia

This term refers to mental decline that's out of line with normal ageing. 'Senile' is really just 'old', but the word has come to refer to mental impairment, distracting us from the fact that ageing and dementia are *not* the same thing. Many different things can cause memory loss and mental disruption. Some can be reversed, while for others there is, as yet, no cure; but the crucial thing to realise is that dementia is not inevitable. Alzheimer's disease may affect around half a million people in the UK alone – yet many more over-65s are simply experiencing natural changes that need to be understood, but can definitely be coped with.

As you go through life, you need to be honest. Are you doing everything you can to make your memory work? Are there aspects of your lifestyle that might be having a negative impact on your brain? Think carefully about your day-to-day life and ask yourself:

- How much do you have to remember these days: more or less than before?

- What is the impact of forgetting? Does it *matter* more or less now?

- When your memory does let you down, how do you respond? Do you ignore it, use it to motivate you, get depressed about it, use it as evidence of a bigger problem …?

When life changes, your experiences of memory are bound to change too. Any problems may lie more with the demands placed on your brain – and the ways you try to tackle them – than with the strength of your memory itself. But if you believe the myths and assume you're going to forget, you'll put in less effort and notice all the mistakes you make, and failure will become a self-fulfilling prophecy.

> **brilliant** tip
>
> As your memory changes and particular tasks become harder, be strategic. Throughout this book you've learnt 'artificial' ways of boosting your natural memory. Things you used to manage effortlessly may now need a bit more support – but that's the whole point. You've got all the strategies you need to make any learning challenge easier, so use them. Make the most of all the tried-and-tested techniques to bolster particular skills, fill in any gaps, and help yourself to stay confident about your memory for as long as you can.

You need to stay alert to any changes, and you must talk to your doctor if you notice particular problems. Maybe there's another health issue affecting your memory? Are you taking medication that could be having side-effects on your thinking? But check too that you're doing the best for your brain: providing it with high expectations and a positive approach, making the most of all the active, engaged learning skills you've been trained to use, and adapting your lifestyle – at every stage of life – to support your brilliant memory.

Physical health

It was the Roman writer Juvenal who came up with the famous phrase *mens sana in corpore sano*: a healthy mind in a healthy body. For a very long time we've known that physical and mental health are closely connected, but it's only in recent years that scientists have begun investigating exactly what that means – looking at specific parts of our diet, for example, to see how the choices we make affect the way our brains form and develop.

Diet

This is another of the many complex aspects of memory. What you eat helps to build your brain, and affects how it operates and whether it keeps working well. But your diet also contributes to your overall wellbeing, which also has a big impact on your ability to think and learn.

The number-one piece of advice is to eat a wide range of nutritious foods in a balanced diet. It's vital to every aspect of your health and wellbeing, which has such a key role to play in mental fitness; but it also means that your brain is getting all the key nutrients it needs to operate at its very best.

Did you know?

It's good to be a fathead. Fats play a number of crucial roles in your brain: in energy reserves, insulation and the conductive connections between cells. They set up the systems for making neurotransmitters, then help to synthesise the neurotransmitters themselves: constructing the systems that let you think and learn, then keeping them working well in the long term.

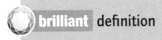 **definition**

Neurotransmitters

These are chemical 'messengers' that let neurons communicate with each other. They're released from stores at the ends of brain cells, then cross the synapses – the spaces between neurons – and attach

> to receptors on the branches of next-door nerve cells, signalling
> them to fire and send out their electrical impulses to other cells.
> They're essential to the connective processes of memory that you've
> learnt to use so well.

To maintain good brain function it's important to keep the fats in your diet in balance: in particular, two essential fatty acids, Omega-3 and Omega-6. Most people in the West consume too much Omega-6, mostly in the form of vegetable oils, and not enough Omega-3 – for which you need to be eating coldwater fish or flaxseed. It can be a significant deficit. Omega-3 fatty acids have wide-ranging benefits for thinking and learning, boosting the brain's speed and connectivity – and also helping to remove some of the emotional barriers to memory like anxiety and anger. Your grandmother was right when she said fish was 'brain food'!

Make sure your diet provides your brain with everything it needs to be brilliant. Here's a selection of some of the most important substances to include, and ideas about where to get them.

Amino acids

Your body takes some specific amino acids from the food you eat and turns them into neurotransmitters, each one with a different function. *L-Glutamine*, for example, in peas, avocado, eggs and peaches, is made into the neurotransmitter GABA, which helps you to stay calm – very important for remembering well. *L-Tryptophan*, from almonds, milk, soybeans and turkey, helps to make serotonin, which in turn can lift your mood and beat depression, removing more potential barriers to memory.

Choline

Another very important neurotransmitter is acetylcholine. It seems to play a key role in making and retrieving memories;

but, as we get older, we produce less, which could be one reason why memory starts to feel harder – and, in severe cases, when actual dementia can set in. It's important to get enough choline in your diet – found in egg yolks, soybeans, eggs and fish – which is converted into acetylcholine in the brain, with the help of …

Pantothenic acid

You can get this, also known as vitamin B5, from beans, fish and whole grains. It also helps to synthesise the red blood cells that carry oxygen to your brain.

The other B vitamins

As well as being vital for overall health, B-complex vitamins are particularly important for the brain. For example:

- B1, found in beans and grains, helps you to concentrate.
- B3, also called *niacin*, found in liver and milk, is important for strong nerve impulses.
- B6, obtained readily from cauliflower, eggs, cod, tuna, bananas, nuts … supports the production of key neurotransmitters. Too little B6 and you'll feel too irritable and tired to learn.
- B9 is also known as folic acid. It helps oxygen to get to the brain and boosts the efficiency of its chemical communications. Folic acid is present in small amounts in many foods, including oranges, broccoli, peas, chickpeas and brown rice, but cooking processes can reduce its effectiveness.
- B12, in cheese, eggs, fish and meat, is involved in making the myelin sheaths that coat your neurons, protecting them and allowing them to conduct electrical impulses.

More vital vitamins

Foods rich in the antioxidant vitamins A, C and E have been shown to boost the memory. These chemicals are found in richly coloured fruits and vegetables: bananas, oranges, red peppers, spinach. They help to mop up substances called free radicals which can cause cell damage in the brain.

Vitamin A helps to shield brain cell membranes from injury. You can get it from egg yolks, fish and green, leafy vegetables.

Vitamin C is important for making neurotransmitters, and is found in fruit like oranges and kiwi-fruit, and vegetables like broccoli and cauliflower.

Vitamin E protects your fatty cell membranes and keeps neurons working well. Dietary sources include eggs, nuts, milk, olive oil and sunflower seeds.

Memory minerals

Iron plays a key role in maintaining good concentration. It's found in red meat, fish, pulses and green vegetables.

Calcium, found in dairy products, leafy green vegetables and tofu, has an important role to play in concentration and learning, helping messages to pass between neurons.

Zinc, from meat, fish, wholegrain bread and soybeans, seems to regulate communications between nerve cells.

Supplementing your success

All of the vitamins and minerals listed above can be found in a balanced and varied diet, but some people like to make sure by taking supplements.

brilliant tip

It's always worth studying the labels to see exactly what you're getting and in what sort of quantities – and finding out which nutrients need to be combined to get the most out of them: for example, vitamin C can help your body absorb iron.

Other supplements have come to be known for their possible memory-enhancing properties.

Ginkgo biloba

For 5000 years the leaves of the ginkgo tree from China, one of the oldest living species, have been used to boost brain function – in particular, memory. The ginkgo is believed to contain compounds that cause small blood vessels – capillaries – to dilate, improving the circulation of blood in the brain.

Ginseng

Another Chinese herb, ginseng, is thought to give the adrenal glands a boost, reducing stress and decreasing the damage done by free radicals.

Brain fuel

Make sure you supply your body and brain with enough energy – and the right sort of energy – to keep working brilliantly.

Don't skip breakfast. The energy you consume first thing in the morning is vital for keeping your brain fuelled throughout the day. Tests with children have shown a significantly higher level of mental performance by those who ate breakfast, compared to those who started the day on empty. Slow-release carbohydrates had the greatest effect on slowing down mental decline during the morning.

Be careful with sugar. A chocolate bar or sugary drink can give your brain a temporary lift, and a surge in instant energy may feel like exactly what you need to achieve a particular task. But the sudden rush of sugar into your blood stream and up to your brain can destroy your concentration and disrupt your thinking, and the high is often followed by an even more noticeable low: a crash in mental and physical energy that can severely hamper your abilities to do *anything*. The trick is to break the cycle of peaks and troughs. In the long run, eating slow-release energy foods – that bowl of porridge at breakfast, those wholegrain sandwiches for lunch – will keep your energy levels stable, helping you to maintain mental focus and fitness, and keeping your brain working at its best. The lower a food's score on the Glycemic Index (GI), the more sustainable its energy is.

Ones to watch

The following substances can have a negative impact on your memory and need to be treated with caution – pleasurable though they may be. Of course it's important to enjoy your food and drink, and many people's lives would be made much worse if they ruled these things out altogether; so the best advice is to be vigilant about any negative effects on your memory, and balance them accordingly.

Salt

As well as being associated with heart disease and raised blood pressure, consuming excessive amounts of salt means that your body depletes itself of potassium. Low potassium can increase anxiety, and anxiety lowers your ability to concentrate – which can cause your short-term memory to falter.

Caffeine

It may stimulate attention and promote concentration, but caffeine can have some less helpful effects on important neuro-transmitters. It lowers adenosine, which is there to help you calm down and sleep, and can also increase the levels of norepinephrine – adrenaline – ramping up your stress.

Alcohol

Alcohol changes your brain's chemistry very quickly. Its effects – short and long term – are complex, ranging from relaxation and mood lifting at one end of the scale to long-term brain damage at the other. Experience will probably tell you that alcohol can disable your memory in many ways: dehydrating your whole system, increasing depression, lowering motivation, hampering decision making, alertness, concentration ... A few drinks may help you relax enough to be creative and funny and confident enough to do some good things with your memory skills, but it's a hard balance to strike.

Did you know?

Around three-quarters of your brain is water. Dehydration can have a rapid and powerful effect on thinking and memory, so it makes sense to keep your brain properly topped up. Sipping water throughout the day will help you to avoid headaches, fend off drowsiness and maintain your concentration.

Speeding up, slowing down

To be mentally active it helps to be physically active – as well as to relax and rest. You'll find it easier to use your memory brilliantly if you get plenty of aerobic exercise, but also know how to wind things down – and leave yourself enough time to get a good night's sleep!

Exercise

Exercise improves your heart's ability to pump oxygen to the brain. It can also release chemicals that make you feel good: happy, confident and motivated to do *everything* well. High-energy sports may be right for you, but don't worry if you prefer something a bit more laid back. New research indicates that walking six to nine miles every week can have a positive effect on the health of your brain. And when you walk you gently stimulate all your key organs, improve your circulation, and give yourself a chance to relax, talk and think.

Did you know?

Organs other than the brain can have an impact on the way you think and learn. If your thyroid gland isn't working properly, for example, the resulting anxiety and lethargy can severely hamper memory. And problems with the pancreas can lead to imbalances of glucose – the only fuel that the brain can use.

And after all that healthy exercise … make sure you know how to rest. Mental down-time is vital to long-term brain health, but it can be a challenge to switch off, especially now that you're using your memory skills so actively during the day.

Relaxation

brilliant tip

Instead of *trying* to relax – which can have the opposite effect, and actually focus your mind on its worries – get into the habit of 'replacing' your stressful thoughts. The trick is to use some reverse psychology. *Try not to think about your left foot.* When you set yourself a challenge like this, it's very difficult to think about anything *other* than your left foot, taking your focus away from the thoughts that were causing you stress. And you can make the most of your memory skills here. Since you've trained your imagination to picture things in vivid detail, why not tell yourself *not* to think about … sitting in a deckchair on a beautiful summer day … the smell of your new baby's skin … what it would be like to live on the moon … You might be surprised at just how easy it is to tempt your brain into rich, immersive thinking – about things that are pleasant, moving, interesting, funny, exciting, calm … anything other than the stressful ideas that were getting in the way of your memory.

Sleep

Good sleep is essential to physical wellbeing and mental fitness, so do everything you can to get enough. There's some fascinating research being done about the exact role of sleep in memory making. It seems that the connections between neurons can be remodelled during sleep, which may explain why babies and young children – with their wealth of new connections – need much more sleep than older people, whose mental connectivity has been reduced. And experiments are showing just how important sleep is in consolidating learning – particularly for skills and procedures. It also seems that sleep has an important job to do protecting new memories from being disrupted by 'interfering' information.

To remember well you need to feel your best – but the good news is that your memory skills can actually help you improve your mood. In general, using your brain actively, really engaging with every challenge and using interesting pictures and funny stories, should help you to feel very positive about your approach to life; but there are also some specific strategies to get more back from your memory. Earlier you learnt how to boost your relaxation and sense of wellbeing by creating a wonderful zone of calm; and now you might like to try some other techniques for letting memory look after you.

Manipulating memories

We know that even our strongest memories are fluid and shifting, a bit different every time we return to them, and liable to end up quite changed from their original form. And yet ... certain memories, very often the ones that bring us problems and pain, can seem stubbornly fixed. These memories tend to be well rehearsed and clearly structured. Every time you think about that hurtful, frightening or embarrassing moment, you see the same mental movie playing out, and it brings back the same negative feelings. So, why not use your trained brain to take back some control? You've proved that you can imagine weird and wonderful things and create powerful artificial memories, so why not use the same skills to reshape some of your real ones?

Here are some of the most important techniques:

Experiment with angles

Does it make things any easier if you see the events from a different point of view – maybe through a more sympathetic pair of eyes? What about watching from far away, putting your small embarrassment into global perspective, or zooming in for a close-up, helping you to understand and accept exactly why something went wrong?

Try resizing key details

You may always have remembered a threatening moment as though you were very small, so try raising yourself up above all the dangers and making all the negative bits of a memory as physically small as possible. On the other hand, it might help more to reduce your role in the scene: to shrink yourself to a size where no one can get to you – or even see you.

See what else makes a difference

You can run your film backwards to understand more about the causes and effects involved. Play around with the speed, slowing down the positive parts and skipping over anything you want to forget. See what happens when you change the volume settings on your memory, maybe giving yourself a loud, confident voice, or decreasing the noise from others. You'll have to see how it works for you and the particular experiences you've stored, but this can be an extremely powerful benefit of memory training: reshaping real memories, then rehearsing the new versions until *they're* the ones that first come to mind.

 **impact**

You can use memory skills to start conquering your phobias. In a calm and safe environment, let your imagination lead you to the source of your fears. Can you pinpoint the moment a particular phobia was created? Think about recent times when your phobia has kicked in. When you've found yourself in your nightmare situation – faced by a spider, trapped in a too-small space – have certain memories always come to mind, fuelling your negative response now? See if the 'memory manipulation' technique works even for memories as firmly fixed and well practised as these. What happens when you change your viewpoint, resize the dangers, alter all the physical sensations and begin imagining different emotional responses? Can you start to make new versions of difficult memories – sufficiently well imagined to change some of your responses and behaviours *now*?

Did you know?

The only fears we're born with are falling and loud noises. Every other kind of fear or phobia needs to be learnt, rehearsed and remembered.

In the zone

Like the top sports stars who train in their imagination, create memories of success before they've even happened. Use your honed visualisation skills to see yourself achieving the performance you want: not just the physical details other people will see, but also the emotional experience that only you will feel. Use all your senses to immerse yourself in this future moment. See yourself from different angles. Imagine the things you'll be able to hear, smell, touch and taste. Go through the event in your mind, focus on the key details that will bring about your success, imagine how you'll cope with any problems, and do everything you can to imagine the feelings of achievement you're determined to enjoy for real.

Return to this 'memory' several times before the real event: the sports meeting, the work presentation, the driving test – whatever you've prepared for in your imagination. Establish it as a memory that you can refer to, draw on it for motivation, and start to expect success – now that you can 'remember' exactly what it's like.

brilliant tip

When things go well in real life – when you do find yourself 'in the zone', at the top of your game – store those memories as powerfully as you can. As soon as possible after the event, explore all the senses and emotions that will fix this moment in your memory. Return to it often, celebrate your success, find motivation here when other challenges seem hard – and use the memory to repeat this particular moment of brilliance again and again.

Use it or lose it

With the right attitude adopted, a supportive lifestyle in place and these new self-improvement strategies at your disposal, you have everything you need to do the most important thing of all: use your memory brilliantly. You've trained your brain to tackle every kind of learning challenge in the most effective way, and you've experimented with examples taken from many areas of life. But now it's about *your* life, and doing it all for real.

The old you

Remind yourself about how you used to think about memory. Look back at Chapter 1 and revisit the responses you gave: about your attitudes to memory, the potential barriers and challenges to making yours any better, and the aspects of it that you most wanted to improve. You imagined what life might be like if you could do the things you wanted to, and *feel* the way you wanted to about your memory. Now it's time to answer all those questions again – and see just how far you've come.

And then …

New targets

Spend a few minutes looking back through the second half of the book, reminding yourself of all the practical applications for your new memory skills – made possible by the way you feel about your memory now. Make some decisions about the ones you're going to try straight away; those that you'll come to in time; and any that you'll have on standby, just in case they're needed. Why not put your money where your mouth is and *memorise* your lists, turning ideas like 'learning names', 'remembering PINs' and 'conquering fears' into images to weave into a story or arrange around a route. Keep coming back to these lists, ticking off the techniques you've started to use, remembering the ones you still need to try – and being ready to activate the strategies on standby.

Reminder rooms

To get into the habit of using your memory skills every day, and to push yourself to 'remember to remember'… build yourself a reminder room. It will save you huge amounts of time and a great deal of frustration – and get you using your memory brilliantly, helping to keep it fit and well.

Choose a real place that you pass by at least a couple of times every day – ideally in the morning and again at night – and create a virtual version of it in your imagination. It might be the cupboard on the landing, a shop on the way to work or a meeting room that you walk past to get to and from your office. Make sure it's big enough for you to stand in (and, shortly, to store things in) but not so big that you can't see it all at once. You need to be able to look into this room whenever you want and see exactly what you've left there. So pick somewhere you can visualise clearly, and spend a few moments fixing it in your mind, using all your senses to make this room or space vivid and real.

To remember the things you have to do, create trigger images and position them carefully in your reminder room – doing everything necessary to make the memories stick.

- If you need to remember to walk the dog, imagine a diamond-encrusted collar and lead handing from a coat-hanger in your landing cupboard.

- To remember to go to the florist's, cover the counter of the newsagent's shop with beautiful flowers.

- When you simply can't forget to phone your Mum on her birthday, picture a huge oil-painting of her hanging over the meeting room table.

Whenever you flash back to the reminder room in your mind, you'll be able to find all the clues you've left for yourself – all fixed there in the most memorable form imaginable: colourful, detailed, exaggerated, funny, strange … Clear connections with you, especially through your feelings (envy at the expensive collar, enjoyment of the sweet-smelling flowers, surprise at seeing your Mum …), will strengthen the memories and speed up the recall, and you'll soon see how easy it is to store many different reminders in your chosen room.

Crucially, you'll be reminded to check your memory room every time you pass the version of it in the real world: the real cupboard, shop, meeting room. Several times a day you'll be prompted to return to your private storehouse and find the images that tell you exactly what you need to do.

 **brilliant** tip

You can add extra image clues for any key details that need to be learnt. Use any other memory systems to give you powerful pictures that will trigger your mind – like the swan that's landed on your Mum's portrait, reminding you to call her at 2 o'clock, or the gerbils crawling through piles of cornflour in the newsagent's, jogging your memory about the flowers you need to buy: *gerbera* and *cornflowers*.

When a job's done, simply imagine its picture being removed from the room: unhooked, cleaned up, painted over … Your brain is remarkably efficient, and you'll soon get used to adding and removing reminders whenever you want. Push yourself to create the most memorable images, following all seven memory-making steps and drawing from as many different memory systems as you can. You'll keep the strategies fresh and your memory skills in great shape, and do your bit to maintain the speed, agility and connective brilliance of your brain.

Good memories

It's important to enjoy memory for memory's sake. Make time to revisit moments from the past that bring you joy – using them to improve your mood and overall sense of wellbeing as well as to keep exercising all your key memory skills.

Remember the police techniques explained in the previous chapter? This is a great opportunity to put them to use again and to go deeper than ever before into some of your happiest memories.

- Bring all your senses and emotions into play as you re-create all the original conditions.

- Pick a key detail as your starting-point and see where the associations take you.

- Imagine studying the scene from different points of view.

- Go backwards through a treasured memory, observing the chain of cause and effect in reverse and enjoying it in a new way – from finish to start!

Even memories you've rehearsed regularly can be reinvigorated in this way. Whether you're actually uncovering more real detail, or *adding* more through the memory process, is up to you to decide. It's an endlessly fascinating exercise to explore your past in this way, and it can give a great boost to your mood and outlook as you revisit the times when you were happiest, re-creating the sensations and feelings in rich and realistic detail. Maybe this amazing ability to travel in time will help you to forgive your memory for the times when, occasionally, it lets you down ...

Chase your dreams

Get into the habit of grabbing on to dream memories as soon as you wake up, then see how long you can keep hold of them. Dreams can be elusive: you know you know what happened in your imagination overnight, but stretching to reach the details seems to push them further away; and the memory traces become fainter after just a few minutes. It's a great way to flex your memory muscles, and it shows you how it feels to catch the most slippery sorts of information.

brilliant tip

Use your dreams to remind yourself just how amazing your imagination can be. Like memory, dreaming changes over your lifetime, is affected by your health and mood, but remains a constant symbol of your incredible, two-sided brain – which is always ready to surprise you with what it can do. So, as you recall key images and events from your dreams, celebrate your mind's ability to conjure up such vivid, oddly logical and richly imaginative ideas. You might even be able to use some of them in your next memory story ...

 **brilliant** recap

- Aspects of memory change with age, but many of the effects can be managed.

- Feed your brain with a balanced diet, supplementing some things, avoiding others.

- Healthy exercise, relaxation and sleep will support your memory skills in the long term.

- You can reshape difficult memories, and use memory to rehearse future success.

- The most important thing you can do for your memory is start using it well, *now*.

Conclusion

Many people talk flippantly about having a 'good' or, more often, a 'bad' memory – as if it's a single thing, something very straight-forward, a possession that you might be lucky enough to have – or not. But when you start thinking about memory, examining your own experiences, reading the research and experimenting with some new ideas, you realise that memory is anything but clear cut. It can't be as simple as saying yours is 'good' or 'bad' because it involves a variety of systems, a complex set of skills, a range of changing experiences. It's anything but straightforward – which means it can be confusing and frustrating, and we might be keen to dismiss it as something out of our control; but, really, this is the best news of all.

It means that you shouldn't be expecting perfection all the time. It means you can't give up on it completely because one bit is letting you down. And it means that you needn't worry about defining your abilities because the next challenge is always around the corner, there are many aspects of memory you haven't even tried yet – and, however you feel about your memory now, there are always things you can do to improve.

Perhaps we've become too reliant on all the electronic memories at our disposal, and stopped noticing just how phenomenally our own brains perform, every minute of every day. Far back in history, people used to celebrate human memory and search for ways to get the most out of it. Now, potentially, we've got the best of both worlds. If we have the confidence, the high aspirations and all the thinking skills required, the memories in our heads can be combined with the gadgets all around us to achieve a whole new level of brilliance.

So keep using your computer, your personal digital assistant – and especially your mobile phone, with all its timesaving functions and clever applications and the whole world of information contained in the SIM. But don't forget what that acronym means – 'Subscriber Identity Module' – because it's a perfect definition of memory itself.

Memory is very much about identity: who you are, how you feel, what you can achieve. As a subscriber you access its benefits, but you also have to know how to use it. The memory module is your brain, and its complexities are responsible for the challenges as well as the infinite possibilities revealed in this book.

When you understand what it means, experience its benefits and find realistic ways to put it to use, your memory, your Subscriber Identity Module, really can change your life.

So start using your whole brain today. Strengthen all your thinking skills, learn the tricks and techniques that will let you remember anything – and look after your memory, so that it will keep looking after you.

By combining ancient techniques with the latest memory aids and using them in your everyday life, you'll see why Mnemosyne, the goddess of memory, was made Mother of the Muses: why memory really is the most important gift of all.

Further reading

Books

The Art of Memory (1992) by Frances A. Yates, Pimlico
The classic text on the history of memory techniques.

The Complete Guide to Memory Mastery (2002) by Harry Lorayne,
   Frederick Fell
Practical tips and techniques from America's most famous
memory man.

Help Your Child to Succeed at School (2010) by Jonathan Hancock,
   Hodder Education
Getting young children into the best habits for remembering and
learning brilliantly.

How To Develop a Brilliant Memory Week by Week (2005) by
   Dominic O'Brien, Duncan Baird Publishers
A year-long memory training programme by an eight-times
World Memory Champion.

The Human Mind (2006) by Robert Winston, Chartered Institute
   of Personnel and Development
Exploring the miraculous mechanisms of the human brain, with
tips for making your own mind do more.

Learning Maps and Memory Skills (2003) by Ingemar Svantesson,
   Kogan Page
Using memory principles to improve your studying, planning,
problem solving and overall creativity.

Memory (2009) by Alan Baddeley, Michael W. Eysenck and
Michael C. Anderson, Psychology Press
An accessible overview of the latest memory research.

The Memory Book (2009) by Tony Buzan, BBC Active
A guide to understanding and using the key memory strategies.

Your Memory – a User's Guide (2004) by Alan Baddeley, Carlton
Books
How your memory works, and how to make it work for you.

Websites

www.bbc.co.uk/sn/tvradio/programmes/memory
Features, resources and links based on a BBC memory project.

**www.bbc.co.uk/science/humanbody/mind/surveys/
memory**
Explore your memory with interactive experiments and tests.

http://www.exploratorium.edu/memory
An online memory exhibition from the San Francisco Science
Museum.

http://helpguide.org/life/improving_memory.htm
A self-improvement website offering information, advice and
support.

www.learningskillsfoundation.com
The latest news about memory and learning, plus details of
projects, publications and public events.

www.memory-improvement-tips.com/exercise.html
A wide range of tools for improving your memory.

http://memoryimprovementcentral.com
Articles on many aspects of memory training.

Index